W9-AKA-328

# ANIMATION LAB
## FOR KIDS

# ANIMATION LAB

**FOR KIDS**

FUN PROJECTS FOR VISUAL STORYTELLING

AND MAKING ART MOVE

LAURA BELLMONT + EMILY BRINK

QUARRY

LONDON PUBLIC LIBRARY

Quarto is the authority on a wide range of topics.

Quarto educates, entertains and enriches the lives of
our readers—enthusiasts and lovers of hands-on living.

www.QuartoKnows.com

© 2016 Quarto Publishing Group USA Inc.
Text © 2016 Laura Bellmont and Emily Brink

First published in the United States of America in 2016 by
Quarry Books, an imprint of
Quarto Publishing Group USA Inc.
100 Cummings Center
Suite 406-L
Beverly, Massachusetts 01915-6101
Telephone: (978) 282-9590
Fax: (978) 283-2742
QuartoKnows.com
Visit our blogs at QuartoKnows.com

All rights reserved. No part of this book may be reproduced in any form
without written permission of the copyright owners. All images in this
book have been reproduced with the knowledge and prior consent of
the artists concerned, and no responsibility is accepted by producer,
publisher, or printer for any infringement of copyright or otherwise,
arising from the contents of this publication. Every effort has been made
to trace the copyright holders and ensure that credits accurately comply
with information supplied. We apologize for any inaccuracies that may
have occurred and will resolve inaccurate or missing information in a
subsequent reprinting of the book.

10 9 8 7 6 5 4 3 2 1

ISBN: 978-1-63159-118-1

Digital edition published in 2016
eISBN: 978-1-63159-186-0

Library of Congress Cataloging-in-Publication Data available.

Design: Debbie Berne
Photography: JUO photography LLC
Shutterstock page 62, 92.

Printed in China

To all of our TGS students:
You make our work good. So good.

# CONTENTS

# PREFACE

One of the best things about meeting new people is telling them what we do for a living. How fun it is to see the excitement, curiosity, and sometimes confusion on their faces when we explain that we teach people art-making through the magic of stop-motion animation. When people ask, as they often do, what stop-motion animation is exactly, it's fun to see their faces light up as we mention *Rudolph the Red-Nosed Reindeer* or *The Nightmare Before Christmas* to help give context for what we have the pleasure of creating with our students, both young and old, on a daily basis here at The Good School.

The questions that follow are some of our favorites. Can children *really* make stop-motion animations? Can they *really* make all of the sets and puppets? Can you teach *me* how to teach my kids? The answer is yes, yes, yes! We wrote this book to help you, the teacher, the parent, guide your child in creating a beautiful and unique work of art that will last a lifetime.

These days, our children are more than "tech savvy." They know their way around smartphones, tablets, apps, and social media. While it is impressive to see such young people engage with the world in this way, we do not want them to lose the ability or desire to make something with their hands using raw materials. When combining the nonlinear, handmade element of creating puppets and sets out of materials like clay, paint, and paper with the more structured, sometimes tech-dependent, process of stop-motion animation, the result is both creative and educational. Whimsical and focused: the perfect combination when working with young people today.

We hope this book guides you through the ins and outs of creating a stop-motion animated film. We hope this book gives you the practical tools to help your kids make the films they want to make. We hope this book gives you the freedom to try new things and to push this medium in new ways. And we hope the process brings you and your children so much joy and pride.

Happy animating!

UNIT
1

# BECOMING AN ANIMATOR

One of the most wonderful things about the art of stop-motion animation is that absolutely anyone can become an animator. By learning the basics and starting with a few simple techniques, every child, every group, can create a unique take on the process. You might even invent something the world hasn't seen yet! For such an old and beloved art form, it's wildly exciting that with stop-motion animation, there's always room for something new.

This chapter reviews the basics to ensure that your stop-motion projects will look as professional as possible, no matter what the subject and which art medium or technology you use to create them.

# THE ANIMATION PROCESS

Let's talk for a moment about animation.

Animation is a movie-making technique that uses a series of . . . anything, really: computer graphics, photographs, drawings, paintings, handmade puppets, or even three-dimensional printed models. Each unit in the series is slightly different from the last so when they are viewed quickly in sequence, there is the appearance of movement. Imagine how flip books work, with each image on the page quickly scrolling to the next.

Another way of describing this process is when you quickly take photos of something in motion. When you scroll back through your camera's photos quickly, there is the illusion of motion.

Stop-motion animation uses the same idea, but the action happens in real life, not constructed in a computer. The elements that are given life through stop-motion animation are often created by hand (or even by computer using three-dimensional printing). Stop-motion animators manipulate their subjects using their hands.

The stop-motion animation filmmaking process is relatively simple. First, you take a still image of a subject. Next, you move the subject a little bit with your hands, completely clear your body/hands out of the area that the camera can see, and capture a new image of your subject in that new position. By continuing to move the subject and capture each new move, in the end you will have a series of images of the subject doing an action in sequence. By playing back through these pictures very quickly, the object appears to be in motion.

There are two main ways that you can string your images together in animated sequence:

1  You can import your still photos from your camera into a photo-editing program like iMovie. In that program, you can adjust the length of time that each picture is shown and add sound, music, and text before saving your finished film.

2  You can connect your camera to a stop-motion animation program during the filming process. These programs automatically string your photos together as an animation and save them as a moving film. Often these software programs come with very helpful features, such as the "onion skin" tool that layers the last photo you took over the one you are about to take so that you can precisely plan your next move.

# TOOLS OF THE TRADE

No matter what style or type of stop-motion animation you're creating—whether two-dimensional or three-dimensional, working with art materials or with your favorite toys—there are a few tools and materials that are great to have on hand.

## Basic Toolkit

Before you start, gather some of these animation must-haves:

- **For cutting:** Scissors, craft knife, cutting mat

- **For drawing and making notes:** Copy paper, pens, pencils, eraser

- **For gluing:** Glue stick and hot glue gun

- **For holding and fastening:** Binder clips, transparent tape, masking tape

*A note about masking tape: As a DIY animator, you can never have too much masking tape! From taping down the legs of your tripod to making sure your puppet doesn't move until you're ready to take a picture, masking tape comes in handy for every project, big or small.*

## Art Supplies

All of the projects in this book involve art supplies. The materials lists give details of what you'll need for each one. Here's an overview of the kinds of materials you'll be working with:

- **Watercolor paints and paper:** Liquid tempera, water-color pan paints, and watercolor pencils on watercolor paper are all great for painting backdrops.

- **Paintbrushes:** A few inexpensive brushes in a range of sizes are handy to have.

- **Sewing supplies:** Thread, sewing and tapestry needles, pins, yarn

- **Fabrics:** For making sets and costumes

- **Beads and buttons:** For fastening, decoration, and eyes (of course!)

- **Non-hardening modeling clay:** To form puppets and props around armatures. We use Plasticine.

- **Wire cutters, needle-nose pliers, and 16-gauge aluminum wire:** For making armatures

- **Wooden drawer pulls and knobs:** These make great feet for puppets and clay figures.

- **Light box:** Not a must-have, but useful when creating a hand-drawn animation or a flip book. The built-in light and flat surface of the box make tracing and copying frames much easier! If you don't have one, you can use a window during the day.

# THE TECH SPECTRUM

There are several animation projects in this book that don't require any technology (see pages 33–59). The results are simply optical illusions of something being animated. If you want to make a stop-motion film using technology, here are a few basic requirements.

- **Camera:** The camera you choose to shoot your animated film depends on the animation editing software you're working with. The various types of animation software—Windows Movie Maker (for PCs), Boinx iStopMotion (for Apple computers), and Dragonframe (for both platforms)—list on their websites which cameras are compatible. (See page 30 for an overview on working with animation editing software.)

If you aren't using animation software to create your film, any digital camera will do. You can scroll through your camera's photos and see them animate right before your eyes! You can also import your photos into a computer and assemble them into a stop-motion animation using iMovie (for an Apple computer) or Windows Movie Maker (for a PC).

- **Tablets and smartphones:** Tablets and smartphones have become fun tools to use for creating stop-motion animations at home. Not only are there free applications that can be downloaded but there are also tripods created specifically for these devices. Animation software, such as iStopMotion, can be used on any Mac product by using the built-in camera to take pictures. The quality won't be quite as great as using a digital camera, computer, and tripod, but using your tablet or smartphone is a great place to start and very user-friendly!

- **Tripods:** Having a sturdy tripod on which to steady your camera, tablet, or smartphone is a huge help! Quality tripods come in all shapes and sizes that vary in price and accessibility. If you are using a high-quality camera, we suggest investing in a high-quality tripod to support your camera. No tripod? No problem! Try putting some masking tape on the bottom of your camera and attaching it to a fixed object like a table or bookshelf. The idea is to make sure your camera is as steady as possible before you start animating.

- **Sound recording equipment:** Using your own voice and original compositions for your animations can really set your film apart! And because most computers, tablets, and smartphones have recording devices already built in, you don't have to spend the extra money on an external microphone. If you would like to upgrade to an external microphone, there are some high-quality options online that are not too expensive. Look for a condenser microphone, with no drivers to install.

# ANGLES AND SHOTS

If you're using technology for your project, a camera (or some other capture device) will be the main tool you use to create your film, so it's very important to pay attention to what your camera's viewpoint is.

Think about how you will use your camera to tell your story. Filmmakers take their audience on a journey by using different views through the camera's lens to explain an idea or lead through a narrative. When you make a movie, you can literally create a window into other worlds. Planning your different camera shots and angles is an important part of the process!

In this book, we define the words *shot* and *angle* as follows:

- **Angle:** The actual angle of the camera as related to its mount on the tripod. For example, when the camera is facing forward, it is called a *straight-ahead angle.* When it's facing down, it is called a *downshoot angle.* For projects that use a downshoot angle, see Unit 3, "Downshoot Animation" (page 61); for projects that use a straight-ahead angle, see Unit 4, "Straight-Ahead Animation" (page 91).

- **Shot:** The way that you shape your scene using camera (or software) tricks like close-ups, wide shots, pans, and so on (defined on pages 19 and 20). Think of it as the viewpoint of the storyteller: a place where you can really play with what the audience sees. Examples of the various types of shots are shown on pages 19 and 21.

## Tips

- Remember, any photos that you take during the shooting of an animation can be used later. Pictures can be copied, pasted, and looped in editing programs.

- Changing your camera angle is a great way to pick up a project where you left off without having to line everything up perfectly from your last session.

- Multiple viewpoints in a film make the movie more fun to watch! Next time you watch a movie, pay close attention to how the story is presented. You'll be in for a treat!

## Shots

- **Pan:** A pan happens when you slowly move the camera either along the horizon or up into the sky along a straight line from one direction to another, taking photos of each incremental change.

- **Zoom:** A zoom means you slowly zoom in the lens so that you can move from a close-up angle to a wide angle or the other way around.

- **Wide:** Great for setting the scene, the wide angle shows a lot of information at once.

- **Medium:** The medium angle still shows a good amount of information, but you can get a glimpse of the details. It's great for capturing conversational moments.

Wide and medium shots

- **Close-up:** A close-up is perfect for highlighting details or showcasing a character's emotions and facial expressions.

- **Extreme Close-Up:** The drama of zooming in!

- **Worm's Eye:** This shot is taken from the ground upward into space.

- **Bird's Eye:** This shot is taken from high above.

- **Over the Shoulder:** This shot is often used to record the back and forth of a conversation or to show a character's unique perspective.

Once you've established how you would like to capture your film, you can begin to plan the best way to tell your story using different angles. Using more than one type of shot will help your stop-motion animation look rich and full, and will also give your viewers an in-depth look at the world you've created. Just remember, be sure to spend enough "animated time" in each of these shots before you move on to the next, ensuring that your audience has adequate time to take in what they are seeing.

Whether you are using a downshoot or straight-ahead angle for your film, it's important to keep your camera steady! Using a tripod or some other clever DIY anchoring technique for your photo-capturing device will let your subjects be the focus of the action; otherwise, the constant motion of your camera can be a distraction.

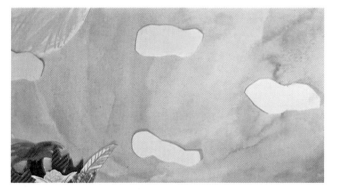

More shot options: (top row)
close-up and extreme close-up;
(center row) worm's eye and bird's
eye; (bottom) over the shoulder

# DESIGNING YOUR FILM

What will you animate with? What kind of "look" do you want to create? What kinds of materials would you like to use? Will you make everything by hand, or will you use found objects? What kind of story do you want to tell? Do you feel inspired by your experiences, art that you have seen in museums, or even something in your own home? Are you inspired by movies? These are all important questions to ask as you go about designing your film. In the animation world, two of the most exciting short film genres are abstract and narrative.

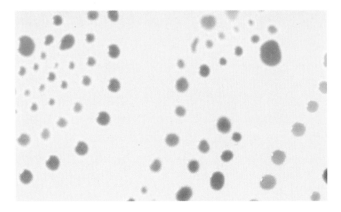

## Abstract films

Abstract films provide a space to truly explore an art medium or a process. Those projects enable children to focus purely on elements of art, such as line, shape, texture, color, and space. Maybe the purpose of the project is to explore a new art-making technique or to simply play with a new material. Either way, the results are sure to be visually striking. The planning for these projects can be minimal; the art happens in the animation!

## Narrative films

Creating a narrative film with children provides a great opportunity to collaborate, design, plan, and execute a real production together as a team. To create a clear story, children have to activate their imaginations, design all the elements of the story (plot, theme, and so on), build their sets and characters, and work together as a team to animate many scenes and animated moments that will go together to create a finished film. They also have to think about the audience watching their finished film. Although telling a story using stop-motion animation is possible with one filmmaker, the work can often be more fully realized with a team.

## Storyboards

Creating storyboards is a great way for kids to simply plan their story and also get a little drawing in! This is a straightforward method to break down each scene and plan for camera shots, select camera angles, and create shot lists (see opposite).

### STORYBOARD CHALLENGE

On a piece of 8½ by 11-inch (21.6 by 28 cm) paper, draw a series of rectangles, each with a few lines to the side. After discussing the different ways of using each camera angle, have children tell a simple story in the most interesting way they can using only the boxes (one for each unique shot). They should draw each moment through the eye of the camera and write a short description of the action on the lines beside the boxes. Remember to keep the exercise story short—for example, a man walks into his home, smells something stinky, and then discovers what it is.

## Script Writing

A super-exciting part of the filmmaking process, script writing can fuse a love for literature with the drama of the stage. Some stories start with a script as the root of the film's inspiration; in other cases, script writing comes after the sets, characters, and storyboards have been created and the story has been completely shot.

## Character and Set Design

Here is a great opportunity to work on those drawing skills and create projects for kids who love to draw. Character and set design are truly one of the most exciting parts of the process! This is the stage where the imagination can run wild. Having kids visually document the look of a character or a set helps create a design that can be used to select materials, plan for scale, and create a cohesive visual feel for the film.

## Shot List

When using animation to tell a story with children, it is extremely important not only to plan the many small moments that will string together to make one story but also to have a vision for the whole. Running through the story, the storyboards, and the script and writing down a list of the necessary shots to capture is an essential way to visually imagine the finished film in its entirety and to make sure that you get all that you need. Take the time to write out a list of essential shots (animated moments) that need to happen to make the story complete. Consider that you *can* shoot your film out of sequence, which might eliminate the trouble of switching out sets and resetting up a scene. Talk to children about the postproduction editing work that will happen and the notion that even though the story will ultimately be told in sequence, the animation process doesn't necessarily have to reflect that order as long as you have your shot lists on hand! This ensures that you won't miss a single scene when in production.

# PIXILATION

Pixilation is an enchanting type of stop-motion animation that turns the lens on the animators themselves! This is the art of animating humans (and other living subjects). The process is the same—making small movements and capturing each one with a camera—and the results are altogether magical.

There are a few wonderful learning objectives inherent to pixilation. The first and the most obvious is the development of both gross and fine motor skills. The movements practiced in the pixilation labs (pages 120 to 131) ask that subjects control their bodies and hold poses for short periods of time. The second is the element of collaboration and teamwork necessary for this style of animation. Nearly impossible (if not hugely difficult) to do alone, this style of stop-motion animation often asks that one or more humans are the subjects and one or more humans operate the capture device, camera, or stop-motion animation software. Filmmaking is, after all, a collaborative art form! Let's get together and make something great!

# ADDING SOUND

One essential part of a great stop-motion animation is adding sound. Your film might call for sound effects, voice-overs, or a musical score. Sound sourcing has traditionally been known as "Foley" and is an amazing process that can lend so much to your film and your filmmaking experience.

Consider the film that you're creating sound for. What kinds of sounds do you imagine in this animation? Make a list of the sound effects you're hoping to record. Stay organized! Now the search begins. Which objects do you have around that could create some of those sounds? Will you make a rhythmic soundtrack or the sound effect for a door closing and opening? Get out there and explore!

All you'll need for this process is a good sound recording device. This could be your smartphone with a recording feature, a more professional-grade recording microphone, or even the built-in microphone in your laptop. Once you have figured out the tech tool that you would like to use to *capture* your sound, you can decide whether you would like to edit or alter it once it is recorded. You can also use sound recording/editing software such as GarageBand (which comes free on Mac computers) or Music Maker Jam (available in app stores for PC/Windows computers) to both capture and manipulate the sound that you record.

It's important to note that using sound recording/editing software isn't necessary if you simply want to record sound and add it to your film. For instance, you could record sound with your smartphone and then import that sound file directly into iMovie or other postproduction editing software, adding it to your video footage directly. With postproduction editing software, however, you have the option to cut a sound clip and line it up with the video to your liking.

# EDITING BASICS

Editing software allows you to import your film and your recorded sound, pair them, arrange them as you would like, and then add text, more sound effects, or music. The first step will be picking the best software for you. Cost and availability might be two big factors that influence your choice. The first thing you will need is access to a computer. iMovie, which comes free on most Mac products, is an easy-to-use editing program. PC users can look for Windows Movie Maker. Final Cut Pro and Premiere Pro (an Adobe product) are fantastic editing and postproduction programs but are a bit pricier and take more time to learn. But once you get the hang of editing, watch out: you will be hooked!

Most editing software that is available today is extremely user-friendly. There are often wonderful user forums and user guides available online should you run into trouble or have any questions about the specific functions of the program.

When you are editing, you might want to consider the following:

- You can start and finish your film with "title cards," or text that introduces the film and closes the film. Often a film starts with the name of the production company or even the title of the film.

- If you need extra animation footage, consider looping moments that you have already recorded or even copying and pasting frames to add to a short clip.

Most editing software allows you to adjust your music so that it can line up perfectly with your animated footage. When you're combining music and video, consider the following:

- Play with how loud your music gets. Remember to keep the music levels low during voice-overs or key sound effect moments.

- Using instrumental music for your soundtrack is a great way to keep the focus on the animation itself.

- A good deal of music out there is protected by copyright. Therefore, it is better not to use music that you don't have permission to use. There are great royalty-free music sites that can be found during simple Google searches. This music is often from the "public domain" and is free and available for use.

# UNIT 2

# OLD SCHOOL
## TRADITIONAL ANIMATION
## TECHNIQUES

This unit will cover some early stop-motion animation techniques that operate *without* relying on technology. A few of them were invented over a hundred years ago, and some are still used in films today! Using simple materials and even some help from Mother Nature, this chapter will take a tour of dazzling tricks of the eye.

# ZOETROPE:
## PICTURES IN MOTION

**A zoetrope** is a great way to introduce and explore the principles of stop-motion animation. You don't need any technology, and it gives kids an opportunity to develop drawing skills and learn how to tell a brief visual story.

## BEFORE YOU BEGIN

These are some measurements to keep in mind, especially if you use a box whose dimensions are different from the one we used.

- The sides of your craft box should be *at least* 1 inch (2.5 cm) high. You can use either the body of a box or its lid to make the zoetrope.

- The length of both sheets of paper, both black and white, should be *at least equal to* the circumference of your craft box.

- The height of the white paper should be *at least* 2 inches (5 cm) and 1 inch (2.5 cm) above the top edge of the box.

- The height of the black paper should be *at least* 4 inches (10.2 cm) and *twice the height* of the white paper.

- If your craft box is larger in diameter than ours, consider using a larger dowel.

## HOW A ZOETROPE WORKS

The term **zoetrope**, which means "wheel of life," was coined by mid-nineteenth-century American inventor William F. Lincoln. His design was one of several cylindrical "moving picture" devices that were developed around the same time. A zoetrope is created by cutting vertical slits into the sides of a cylinder. On the cylinder's inner surface is a band of sequential images. When the cylinder is spun, it creates the illusion of motion as the viewer looks through the slits at a rapid progression of the images.

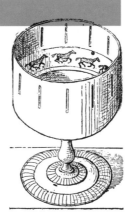

★ TECH-FREE PROJECT

## MATERIALS

Note: *See "Before You Begin," left, for measurement information.*

- Tape measure
- Round papier-mâché craft box, 4" (10.2 cm) in diameter and 12½" (31.8 cm) in circumference
- Craft knife
- Cutting mat
- 1 sheet each of heavyweight paper in white and black
- Ruler
- Glue stick
- Scratch paper
- Pencil
- Scissors
- Markers
- Wooden dowel at least ½" (1.3 cm) in diameter
- Hot glue gun

## ACTION!

**1** Measure the circumference of your craft box. Cut both sheets of paper so their length is equal to the box's circumference. Cut the white sheet to a width of at least 1 inch (2.5 cm) higher than the box's top edge and the black sheet to a width of at least twice the height of the white one. Lay the white paper over the black paper and use the glue stick to glue them together along one edge (fig. 1). You'll draw your sequential drawings on the white paper; the black paper will serve as the viewing mask.

**2** Consider what you want to show in your sequence: A flower growing? A door opening? A cat turning into a butterfly? The sequence will form a "loop" that starts and ends at the same place. Next, think about how many drawings you want to include. If you use a box the same size as ours, plan for at least 10 individual images. Sketch your ideas on scratch paper first. Once you've decided on the number of images, measure and mark the same number of spaces exactly equidistant along the top edge of the black paper. At each mark, cut a slit 2 inches (5 cm) deep and ¼ inch (6 mm) wide. The slits should almost meet the top edge of the white paper (fig. 2).

**3** Draw your images in the correct sequence on the white paper. Position each image directly under its corresponding slit, making sure it's centered beneath it (fig. 3).

**4** Measure and mark the circumference of the dowel on the box on the bottom. Cut a hole into the box so the dowel fits it tightly (fig. 4).

**5** Roll the paper slightly to fit it inside the box. The images should be inside the box and facing inward, with the slits at the top (fig. 5).

**6** Use the hot glue gun to attach the paper to the inside of the box (fig. 6).

**7** Use the hot glue gun to adhere the dowel to the bottom of the box (fig. 7).

**8** Spin your zoetrope quickly by turning the dowel between your palms (fig. 8). Peer through the slits at the top to view your short tale of transformation!

**fig. 1.** Cut both sheets of paper to the same length as your box's circumference. Glue the white sheet to the black sheet, aligning them along one edge.

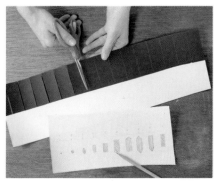

**fig. 2.** Measure and cut evenly spaced slits along the top edge of the black paper.

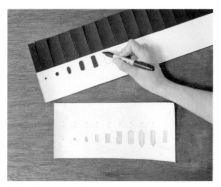

**fig. 3.** Draw each image in the sequence directly under and centered beneath each slit.

**fig. 4.** Measure, mark, and cut a hole to fit the dowel into the bottom of the box.

**fig. 5.** Position the images inside the box.

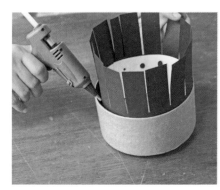

**fig. 6.** Glue the paper in place.

**fig. 8.** Spin the zoetrope and watch the pictures move!

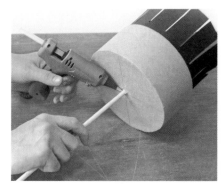

**fig. 7.** Glue the dowel in place.

# CLAY-PAINTED
# ZOETROPE

**If you thought** the zoetrope couldn't get any cooler, then think again! In this lab, we introduce you to one of our favorite techniques, clay painting, to create a completely unique zoetrope. We'll be using most of the instructions from Lab 1 to make this zoetrope, but please be aware of a few important changes noted below.

## BEFORE YOU BEGIN

See the notes on page 35 for Lab 1, but also consider these differences:

- For this lab, you should use a heavier weight paper (such as watercolor paper) for the lining of the box so that it can support the weight of the clay.

- You will be using layered clay to create the images on the inside of the zoetrope rather than drawing.

★TECH-FREE PROJECT

## MATERIALS

Note: *You'll need all the materials listed on page 35 for Lab 1, plus:*

- **For the heavyweight white and black papers:** *We suggest using watercolor papers for this zoetrope.*

- **Hot glue gun:** *Use instead of a glue stick to glue the papers together.*

- **Non-hardening modeling clay in several colors**

- **Spearing implement, such as a toothpick**

# ACTION!

1  See Step 1 on page 36 for measuring the box and cutting the white and black paper to fit its circumference. Use the hot glue gun to glue the white sheet to the black one along one edge (fig. 1).

2  Determine how many incremental drawings you would like to feature in your zoetrope. Consider what you will be transforming in your drawings. We recommend sketching and planning your ideas on scratch paper first. You may choose an action that's more literal or narrative, but we also suggest trying something more abstract with the modeling clay. We recommend planning for at least 10 individual images. Keep in mind that the image sequence will ultimately form a loop, starting and ending at the same place.

3  Once you have decided how many images you will feature, see Step 2 on page 36 for information about planning and measuring their spacing.

4  Measure the circumference of the dowel and mark a spot directly in the center of the box bottom. Cut a hole that closely fits the dowel.

5  Begin applying your modeling clay, which is made of oil and wax. It is very important to use only small bits of clay so your zoetrope doesn't become too heavy (fig. 2). Use a spearing technique to form your small bits of clay into a small picture.

6  Remember to create each transitional moment directly under each slit, trying to keep the spacing between each as even as possible. Place the clay paintings along the upper portion of the white paper positioned just below each slit (fig. 3).

7  Using the hot glue gun, attach the joined pieces of white and black paper to the inside of the box with the images facing inward and the slits at the top (fig. 4).

8  Next, use the hot glue gun to adhere the dowel to the bottom of the box, protruding from beneath.

9  Watch the magic! By turning the dowel between your palms, you can spin your zoetrope quickly while peering through the slits at the top to view your short tale of transformation.

**fig. 1.** Use a hot glue gun to attach the white paper to the black paper, as these papers are a heavier weight.

**fig. 2.** Here is an example of how you might smear your clay onto your paper.

**fig. 3.** Place the clay along the top of the white paper and just below each slit.

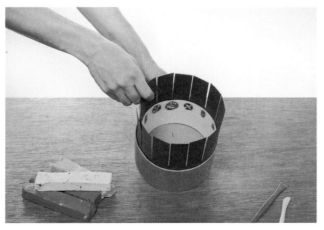

**fig. 4.** Carefully fit your paper into the box so that it can be glued in place.

# LAB 3

# STICKY NOTE
# FLIP BOOK

**Oh, how we love flip books!** Not only are they low-maintenance and inexpensive, but they're also a great way to work on drawing skills and at the same time teach the basics of stop-motion animation.

## BEFORE YOU BEGIN

- Thinner paper allows the artist to see a trace of the drawing underneath, making it easier to draw a continuing image.

- Thicker paper makes for easier flipping of the pages.

- It is really important that you keep the drawings in sequence. Numbering the back of the pages in pencil is a good way to keep the drawings in order.

- The more frames (pages) a flip book has, the smoother the animation will appear. With fewer pages and larger changes in drawings, a flip book will appear fast and choppy.

- Anywhere from 15 to 24 frames per movement will make for a good range of motion.

★TECH-FREE PROJECT

## MATERIALS

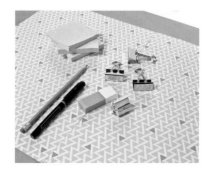

- Computer paper, a stack of sticky notes, or tracing paper, cut into the same size sheets

- Pencil, pen, or marker

- Binder clips, stapler, masking tape, or hole punch with string to tie the flip book together

# ACTION!

1 Assemble your sheets of paper into a clean stack. Remember to number the back of each page in pencil so you can keep your drawings in sequence (fig. 1).

2 Come up with a subject you would like to animate. This can be as simple as a bouncing ball or as complicated as a human walking.

3 Start drawing on the very bottom sheet of the stack (fig. 2).

4 Once the first drawing is finished, turn to the next page (second page from the bottom) and draw your subject again, slightly moving its position if you desire motion in the flip book, or draw it in the same place to keep it still. Remember, big changes in the drawing will make for a quick, choppy motion, while small changes will appear smooth when flipping.

5 Continue this process and draw through all of the pages until you are finished.

6 Using binder clips, a stapler, masking tape, or a hole punch and string, bind one edge of your stack of drawings. This enables you to flip and flip and flip!

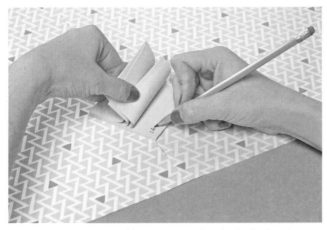

**fig. 1.** Stack your pages and be sure to number the back of each one so they stay in order.

**fig. 2.** Begin drawing from the back of the book, not the front.

# PAINTED
# FLIP BOOK

**Are you ready to take your flip book to the next level?**
This exciting tech-free project introduces paint and encourages you to work on a much bigger surface! The results are totally unpredictable and totally cool. Have fun!

## BEFORE YOU BEGIN

- Even though we are working with large paper, you want to make sure the stack is easy to flip. That is the whole point, right? We suggest keeping your pages around 8½ by 11 inches (21.6 by 28 cm).

- It is important that you keep your paintings in sequence. Numbering the back of the pages lightly in pencil is a good way to keep the drawings in order.

- Be sure to tape down the edges of your paper when painting so that they don't warp while they are wet.

- The more frames (pages) a flip book has, the smoother the animation will appear. With fewer pages and larger changes in drawings, a flip book will appear fast and choppy.

- Anywhere from 15 to 24 paintings will make for a good range of motion.

★TECH-FREE PROJECT

## MATERIALS

- Heavy watercolor paper, 8½" x 11" (21.6 x 28 cm) or 9" x 12" (23 x 30.5 cm)
- Pencil
- Scratch paper
- Masking tape
- Watercolor or acrylic paints
- Paintbrushes
- Binder clips, stapler, masking tape, or hole punch and string

# ACTION!

1 Assemble your sheets of paper into a clean stack. Remember to number the back of the pages in pencil so you can keep your drawings in order.

2 Come up with a subject you would like to animate. This could be something inspired by a story, or you could use the paint and try something more abstract and loose. No matter what, it will look great when it's in motion! Draw out your ideas on scratch paper.

3 Tape the paper to your work surface (fig. 1). Start painting on the very bottom sheet of the stack.

4 Once the first painting is finished, turn to the next page (second page from the bottom) and paint again, slightly moving its position if you desire motion in the flip book, or paint it in the same place to keep it still. Remember, big changes in the painting equal a quick, choppy motion, while small changes will appear smooth when flipping.

5 Continue this process, painting all of the pages until you are finished (fig. 2).

6 Once the painted pages are dry and you have carefully removed them from the tabletop by peeling off the masking tape, it's time to bind your flip book! You might need something a little heavier with your heavyweight paper. Using binder clips, a stapler, masking tape, or a hole punch and string, bind one edge of your stack of paintings.

**fig. 1.** Taping the paper to your work surface will keep the paper from buckling while it dries.

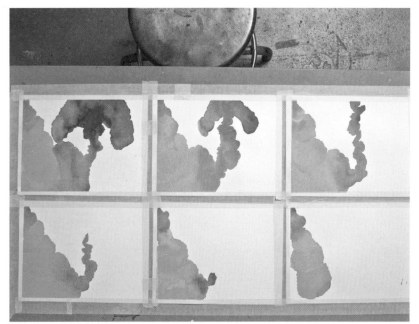

**fig. 2.** Paint the pages in sequence to best plan the changes.

# SUN-PRINTED LEAVES
# FLIP BOOK

This lab is a great opportunity to go outside and explore your world, with the mission to create images and string them together in the form of a flip book. You'll also use the fun and easy technique of sun printing.

This process allows for trips foraging for plant material outside. What a great way to explore your neighborhood or even just your backyard! Once you've found your organic "subjects," play with this simple and exciting photo-art material.

## BEFORE YOU BEGIN

- We will be creating at the very least 15 individual pages for this flip book. As with earlier flip books, the more pages, the better!

- Do you want your plants to appear to be growing or shrinking in your flip book? Think about what you want to show, and then find plants that are similar shapes but different sizes so you can arrange them in order of smallest to largest or vice versa.

- The blue molecules on the photo paper are sensitive to ultraviolet light and will develop when placed in the sun. For best results, remove the paper from the package and arrange the leaves on the paper in a relatively dark place to avoid exposing the paper until you are truly ready (see below).

## MATERIALS

Note: *Be sure to purchase a package of sun-sensitive photo paper that has at least 15 sheets inside. Ideally, this lab should use 15 to 30 pages per flip book.*

- Small leaves or small plants
- Sun-sensitive photo paper (Common brands are NaturePrint and SunArt.)
- Cardboard cut slightly larger than the sun-sensitive photo paper
- Stickpins
- Clock or stopwatch
- Shallow tub for water
- Drying rack
- 2 binder clips

**1** Arrange your foraged plants in an interesting sequence on a tabletop, perhaps from smallest to largest to show the plant growing.

**2** Remove five sheets of photo paper from their sun-protected package and pin them to the pieces of cardboard using stickpins inserted at each corner (fig. 1).

**3** Working quickly, arrange the first five laid-out plant sequences onto the pages (fig. 2).

**4** Now it is time for some sun! Choose a sunny spot and lay your cardboard/paper panels out. Once your paper on cardboard sheets are arranged in the sun, start the clock. The exposed areas of photo paper will change from blue to white. When you see the color of the paper completely turn white, your paper is likely ready. (Note: Each brand of photo paper might have a slightly different sun exposure time, so be sure to consult the package. Most recommend a sunning time of about 2 minutes.)

**5** Time for a water bath to stop the developing. Place your five sheets in the shallow tub filled with water and make sure they are completely submerged (fig. 3). Watch the white turn to blue, and then the blue will turn to white! This setting period can take from 1 to 5 minutes (again, consult the package of the specific brand of paper you are working with).

**6** Lay the finished sheets on a drying rack to dry.

**7** Repeat steps 2 to 6, using five new sheets from the light-protected pack, at least two more times to fill 15 pages for your flip book.

**8** Once all the pages have dried, arrange your beautiful photo prints in sequence and bind them at one end with two binder clips.

**9** Now flip (fig. 4)! What a beautiful, organic sequence of prints in motion!

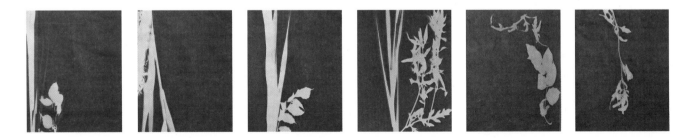

**fig. 1.** Pin the sun-sensitive photo paper to the cardboard sheets.

**fig. 2.** Arrange the plant subjects on the mounted paper.

**fig. 3.** Soak the paper in a tray of water to stop development.

**fig. 4.** Flip the pages to see the leaves move.

# LAB
# 6

# DRAWING
# CARTOON CELS

This lab introduces a classic cartoon technique that is still used in many animations that you see today. This lab is great for those who love to draw and want to work on hand drafting skills while exploring stop-motion animation.

## BEFORE YOU BEGIN

What is your favorite cartoon character? Do you love to draw? How long can you draw the same thing again and again? How does an object change when it moves through space? Using simple art materials, an illuminated window, and drawing and redrawing your subject again and again, you can bring your favorite characters to life!

★TECH-FREE PROJECT

## MATERIALS

- Graphite pencil and eraser
- 20 to 50 sheets of tracing paper cut to the same size, ranging from 5″ x 5″ (12.5 x 12.5 cm) to 8½″ x 11″ (21.6 x 28 cm)
- Light box or illuminated window (of durable glass/plastic)
- Masking tape
- Sketch paper
- Pens
- Ruler (optional)
- Binder clips or paper clips

1   Using a pencil, number the back of each page of tracing paper so that you can keep them in sequential order.

2   Either use a light box or find a window that is heavy and safe enough to withstand a light amount of pressure. Holding up your first piece of tracing paper against the surface of the light box or window, use two pieces of masking tape on each corner to mark the top two edges of the page (fig. 1). This will serve as your guide each time you add another sheet of tracing paper to the light box or window.

3   Now plan your action. Will this hand-drawn animation feature a bouncing ball (originally used in early animation experiments called "The Ball Test")? Will you morph one thing into another? Will you make a cartoon character complete a simple action? Take a moment to sketch out your idea, even using the same page. Once you have an idea of the action you would like to capture, you can jump into drawing.

4   Holding your first sheet of tracing paper up to the masking tape template on the window, draw your first scene. You can use pen or pencil.

5   Layer the second sheet *on top* of the first. This enables you to see the former drawing so that you can redraw it in a slightly different position. A ruler can help you measure how much each image moves from one page to the next.

6   Once you have layered three pages, carefully remove the bottommost (stacking it neatly in sequential order to the side) and add another to the top (fig. 2).

7   Continue to stack new pages and draw a slightly different action on each new page. Explore motion and what can happen when you change the quality of the line slightly for each new drawing. Be sure to keep your finished pages in the correct order!

8   Once the main action has been completed, it can be fun to go back into your drawings to add details or even to flesh out the space on the page that is *around* the action. (Note: These drawings can eventually be turned into real moving stop-motion animations should you encounter a camera in the future. Hang on to them, because you never know!)

9   When you have finished your drawing sequence, clip them together so that they can remain a unit until you would like to animate them (fig. 3), display them, share them, or work back into them at a future time!

**fig. 1.** Create guidelines on the window with masking tape to show where to line up your drawings.

**fig. 2.** Always keep three layers of drawings on the window!

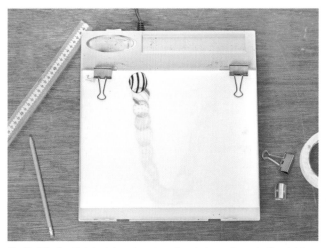

**fig. 3.** Clip the finished drawings together to keep them in the right sequence.

# KIRSTEN LEPORE

Kirsten Lepore is a director and animator based in Los Angeles, with an MFA from CalArts. Her films have taken top prizes at SXSW, Slamdance, the Stuttgart Festival of Animated Film, the Florida Film Festival, the Arizona International Film Festival, the Vimeo Festival + Awards, the Annie Awards, and many others. She has given presentations everywhere, from Pixar to Portugal, and has also been featured in *Juxtapoz Art & Culture Magazine, SHOTS Magazine, Animation Magazine*, and *Focus Features*, and was named one of the fifty most creative people by *Creativity* magazine. With a client list that includes Google, MTV, Cartoon Network, *Yo Gabba Gabba!*, *Newsweek*, Whole Foods, Toyota, Facebook, Nickelodeon, Nestlé, and *Glamour* magazine, Kirsten has had her work featured on TV, on the Web, in museums, and at international film festivals. To see more of her work, visit www.kirstenlepore.com.

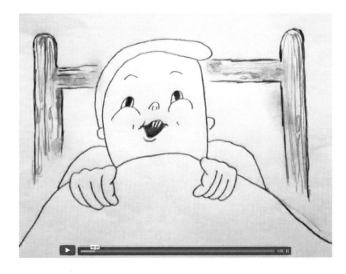

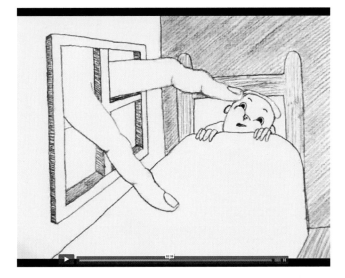

(This page and opposite) Stills from *Story from North America,* an allegorical tale about respect for life and the environment. Directed and animated by Kirsten Lepore and Garrett Davis, who also wrote and performed the music.

UNIT

# 3

# DOWNSHOOT ANIMATION

Animating with your camera facing down toward a tabletop or flat surface is one of the most effective ways to create stop-motion animation. From the perspective of the camera, your animation stage still has a top and a bottom (or sky and ground) and can appear very dimensional, while the animator can easily and methodically move items around on a flat surface, where puppets aren't affected by gravity.

This camera position also allows for great freedom in experimenting with materials and some classic fine art–based approaches to making animation. In this chapter, we explore methods used to create sets and characters for a narrative film and try our hand at some methods that focus on the material itself and what's possible when it comes to life beneath the lens!

# DOWNSHOOT CAMERA ANGLE

The downshoot angle is used for a wide range of animation techniques, from two-dimensional animation and three-dimensional animation to pixilation (see page 26) and multiplane animation (see opposite).

In a downshoot (or "two-dimensional") angle, the camera is pointed down toward the ground, a tabletop, or any other flat surface. One of the best things about down-shoot animation is that you don't have to fight against gravity. In a world where puppets need to hold precarious poses in space until their picture is taken, gravity is *not* our friend. By placing puppets and sets on these flat surfaces, the downshoot angle creates the illusion of top and bottom (that is, the sky and ground); is ideal for swimming, running, and flying movements; and can incorporate many types of puppets and art media.

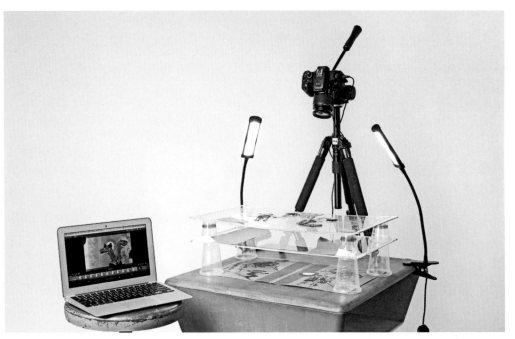

You can film a downshoot project with either a camera or a smartphone. If you're shooting with a smartphone camera, use a flexible tripod (right), which will make it easy to shoot from that angle.

## Creating a Downshoot Set

Here's what you'll need to create a set for your downshoot animation projects:

- **Film stage:** A no-frills table with a top measuring at least 24 by 12 inches (61 by 30.5 cm) should give you enough room for a basic shooting set. Cover the top with a piece of plexiglass or some other protective covering if you want to avoid damaging it.

- **Lighting:** You'll need at least two direct light sources to make sure the lighting on your set is balanced. An inexpensive pair of clip-on LED lamps will do the job nicely. Be mindful of overhead light shining behind an animator. It can cast unwanted shadows in the animation.

- **Multiplanes:** Multiplanes are sheets of plexiglass that are stacked with space between each sheet to give you more than one plane on which to work and create the illusion of depth (see below).

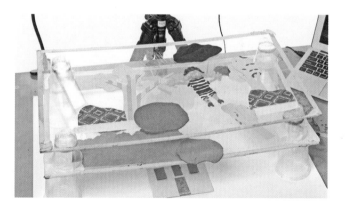

### MULTIPLANES 101

The multiplane lets the animator work on a flat surface, which frees you from the challenge of negotiating with gravity. The stack of plexiglass allows you to create a deeper visual space that includes a foreground, background, and midground. This stack (from two layers all the way up to twenty in some cases!) is positioned directly beneath the lens of the camera, visually creating a multidimensional space and an illusion of depth.

Plexiglass can be cut to size at your local picture-framing store. (Note: Freshly cut plexiglass can sometimes have sharp edges, so be sure to carefully line them with masking tape before using them with children.) Stack the plexiglass sheets on top of each other, separated at the four corners with a sturdy object holding up each corner to create space between. We love to find creative ways to put space between our stack of planes. One of our favorite methods is to use small disposable plastic cups that can be stacked to a preferred height and taped together. As long as each layer is lifted the same amount on all four corners, you're in good shape! If you can't make it to the framing store for plexiglass, take the glass out of a picture frame you have in your house. Be sure to put masking tape around the sides and corners so you don't cut yourself!

Remember that when you're animating on a multiplane, lighting can become a very important tool. Try using lights to illuminate different levels of your multiplane.

# LOOSE AND MESSY
# CHARCOAL

**This lab explores the messy fun of charcoal** and its potential to create beautiful, abstract stop-motion animated shorts! By using all of the traditional methods that masters might use when creating works of fine art made with charcoal, the animator is able to explore the material while capturing these exciting changes under the lens!

- As with our other downshoot animation setups, thoroughly tape down your first sheet of heavyweight drawing paper on all sides using masking tape.

- Remember, you will be rubbing and erasing—perhaps vigorously—so you should have a very stable piece of paper to work upon.

## MATERIALS

- Several sheets of heavyweight drawing paper
- Masking tape
- Vine charcoal
- Stick charcoal
- Camera or other capture device
- Tripod
- Smudging tools
- Kneaded erasers

# ACTION!

**1** Start making small, simple marks on the paper with the charcoal and capture each small change with a photo as you go.

**2** Experiment with using the charcoal tools in different ways, smearing and smudging your marks (fig. 1).

**3** Try erasing sections of your drawing (fig. 2).

**4** Try some of the following prompts to explore the potential of charcoal in animation. You can choose to change your paper for each new exercise, or you can build and build on one page.

■ Explore as many different marks as you can using the same tool. What happens when you use the side of a charcoal stick as opposed to the end? Can you fill the entire page with different marks? This exercise will create a blossoming effect.

■ Try slowly filling up the page with soft, sweeping marks using the side of the charcoal stick. Keep building and building until the page is full. Now try removing marks with an eraser.

■ Draw a scene on a new piece of paper using charcoal. Fill the page with drawing. Perhaps you will draw from life, or maybe you will create an entirely new reality! Select one area of the drawing that you would like to come to life. Maybe this is a fish in a fishbowl? Perhaps it is a curtain fluttering in the breeze? By erasing and redrawing, change the image a tiny bit for each picture. Experiment with keeping some areas still while others come alive.

**fig. 1.** Try smearing and smudging the charcoal.

**fig. 2.** Erase parts of your drawing for a cool effect.

# RIPPING AND CUTTING
# COLORED PAPERS

**This lab is such fun** for adults, children, and really little ones who are practicing their fine motor skills. It uses simple construction paper as its core material. The animator is able to visually leave the one-dimensional realm and stack, cut, and tear to create almost sculptural elements that literally appear to be jumping out of the page!

## BEFORE YOU BEGIN

Consider that you will slowly be revealing each new layer under the lens while you are planning your color sequence. For example, would you like to see red revealed underneath green? Should black give way to white?

## MATERIALS

- Pack of multicolored construction paper, either 8½" x 11" (21.6 x 28 cm) or 11" x 17" (28 x 43.2 cm)
- Stapler
- Masking tape
- Scissors
- Camera or other capture device
- Tripod
- Craft knife

## ACTION!

1   To get started, select a stack of multicolored construction paper, layering different colors on top of each other.

2   Once you have stacked 10 to 15 sheets of paper, staple them together on one end and tape that stapled end securely to the tabletop. Set up your camera and tripod. Now you are ready to animate!

3   Use scissors to create a hole in your topmost piece of paper (fig. 1).

4   Next, capturing each new move using your camera and/or stop-motion animation software, make larger tears in the topmost piece to reveal the paper beneath. Tear more away and then tear from the next sheet to reveal still more below (fig. 2).

5   Remember that your tools will create different visual effects. Hand tearing makes for a lovely organic edge (fig. 3). Scissors can be used for clean cuts. Craft knives can be used (delicately!) to break into new layers in a very precise way.

6   Try some of these exercises to explore what is possible through this method:

■ Use your hands to tear your paper away from a center point in the topmost sheet of paper. As you capture each new move and as the center point expands, begin to tear away from the center point of the next sheet of paper in the stack. Continue until there is nothing left to tear!

■ Experiment with ripping away from an edge in clean, straight lines. This method is great with scissors.

■ Get sculptural! Following the model of the first exercise above, rip away a shape rather than just a center hole. This way you can emulate this unique shape from layer to layer, repeating it smaller and smaller on different colors of paper (fig. 4).

**fun looping tip**  Once you have captured these sequential images, you have the photos to play with! Using either your animation software or after importing your sequential images into a postproduction editing software (such as iMovie), you can line up your photos in sequence and then line them up again in reverse! This creates a loop that shows the paper ripping apart and then almost healing itself. This loop can be played infinitely, creating a very beautiful and hypnotic short film!

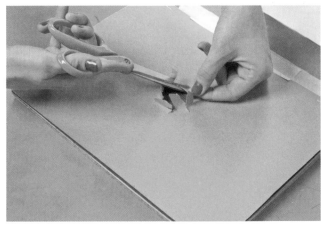

**fig. 1.** Scissors make an easy access hole into your first page.

**fig. 2.** Cut and tear the layers underneath.

**fig. 3.** Tearing the edges of the paper by hand makes an organic, natural shape.

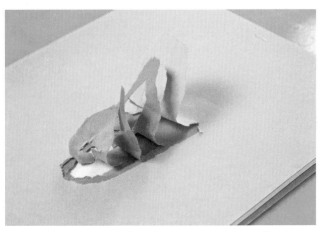

**fig. 4.** Tear away the same shape but in progressively smaller sizes from each layer of paper.

# SMEARING AND SMUDGING
# CLAY

**Claymation is a favorite** of all the stop-motion animation techniques. Not only is clay great fun to work with, but it also finds a perfect home in stop motion because it's super easy to manipulate and holds its shape while you capture each little change! In this lab, you'll experiment with claymation to create beautifully fluid and abstract animated shorts. Clay also provides an opportunity to develop fine motor skills and explore some elements of art: shape, form, color, space, and texture.

## BEFORE YOU BEGIN

Be sure to tape your paper down well! Remember that you will be pushing clay around—in some cases, with a bit of pressure—and you want the clay to be moving, not the animating surface!

## MATERIALS

- Camera or other capture device
- Tripod
- Heavyweight drawing or watercolor paper
- Masking tape
- Multicolored non-hardening modeling clay
- Clay sculpting tools
- Pencil (optional, to be used as a sculpting tool)

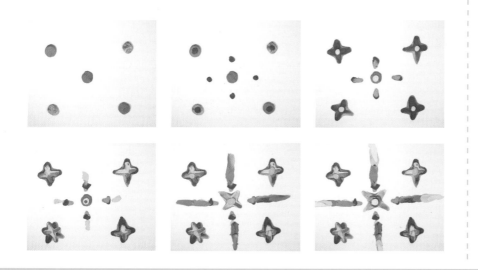

# ACTION!

1   Set up your camera facing in the "downshoot" position and secure your first sheet of paper to the tabletop with masking tape. Then try the following techniques.

2   Swirl: Start with one color of modeling clay as your base. You can create the base under the lens by adding clay a little bit at a time and capturing photos of each new addition until you have covered a significant area. Start pushing the clay in an arching/circular motion using your fingertip or the flat side of a clay sculpting tool. As you move the clay in this swirling motion, add tiny bits of a contrasting color into the swirl and smear. Keep adding and swirling to create an amazing spiral of shifting colors (fig. 1).

3   Expand and contract: Again, after creating a solid clay base (as described above), gradually create a small mound, capturing each slight change as you go. Create a small opening and slowly, picture by picture, stretch that opening to expand outward (fig. 2). You can show the images in reverse to make the opening contract.

4   Smearing waterfall: This activity is inspired by impressionist paintings and uses a bright palate to create beautiful smeared, flowing animations. It also helps simplify the process for very young animators practicing their fine motor skills. It could even serve as a space to learn more about color mixing and color theory. Using a piece of heavyweight paper that is taped down very well, choose one color of modeling clay and create small, smeared smudges on the paper. Now begin animating and capturing a photo of each incremental change as you go. While continuing to smear and add to your original trail of clay, play with adding new colors to that smear and even creating new smears all over the page (fig. 3)! Experiment with adding primary colors on top of other primary color fields, mixing them together to create a new secondary color. The result will appear as a flowing stream of morphing and transforming clay.

5   Create an abstract design by building up layers and shapes (fig. 4).

**fig. 1.** Create a swirl of colors by adding new pieces of clay and smearing it with your fingertip.

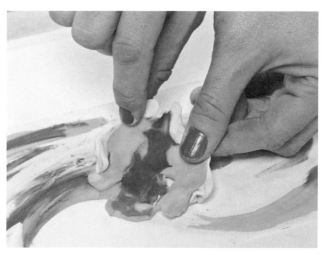

**fig. 2.** Pull out the mound of clay to create an expanding opening.

**fig. 3.** A clay sculpting tool makes a flowing waterfall effect.

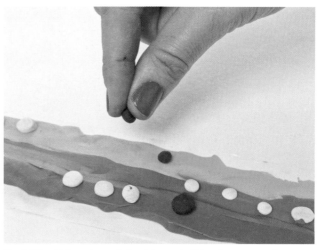

**fig. 4.** The sticky nature of clay lets you build up layers to make a design.

# DRIP DROP
# WATERCOLOR

**This lab is a fun and freeing way to experiment** with mixing color, animating movement, and exploring the beauty and freedom of experimental abstract animation. The jewel-like effect of these illuminated beads of water is just enchanting!

## BEFORE YOU BEGIN

- Just as with any other downshoot or multiplane shot, it is really important that you take your time in the setup! Make sure that your backdrop paper is aligned correctly by consulting the viewfinder on your camera or animation software view. Tape down the backdrop paper securely. Secure the plastic cups (or alternative spacers) to the multiplane and secure the whole combination to the tabletop. Tape it all down!

- Now let's talk lighting. One of the most magical qualities of this lab is the visual effect of the watercolor drops appearing almost luminescent and jewel-like. This is made possible by the strategic addition of lights shining up from beneath the multiplane. Experiment with lighting and see if you can create a lovely luminous environment!

## MATERIALS

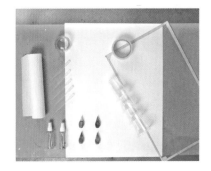

- Camera or other capture device
- Tripod
- Large piece of watercolor paper for backdrop
- Masking tape
- Plastic cups or other same-height spacers to lift the multiplane
- Sheet of plexiglass (for a multiplane)
- Bendable lights (see "Before You Begin")
- Food coloring
- Glasses or cups for water and color mixing
- Eyedroppers
- Paper towels

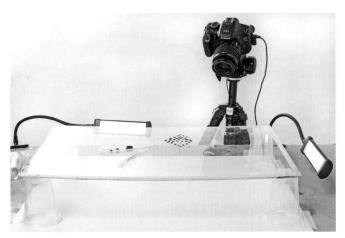

Lighting and multiplane setup

# ACTION!

1 Using the simple primary colors that come in most food coloring packs, create a range of colors that you would like to animate with! Squeeze a few drops of food coloring into cups filled with a bit of water. Experiment and play. How saturated do you want your color drops to be? Perhaps then you might want less water in your cup. If you want a lighter color, add more water.

2 Using the eyedropper, squeeze a bit of color from your selection and carefully place one drop at a time on top of the multiplane. The plexiglass surface allows for easy application and easy removal of each application using a paper towel. Capture each new addition with your camera (or alternative capture device) and/or animation software.

3 Place one drop down (fig. 1), take a picture, wipe it away (fig. 2), and replace a new drop in a slightly different direction. This will have the appearance of a water drop on the run!

4 Try changing colors as you go (fig. 3)!

5 Experiment with different shapes beyond the simple round water drop. Can you create larger and more organic moving shapes? Using more water on top of the multiplane will also allow for some fun with color mixing/spreading under the lens. A larger blob of water with a little bit of color added can be quite magical, too.

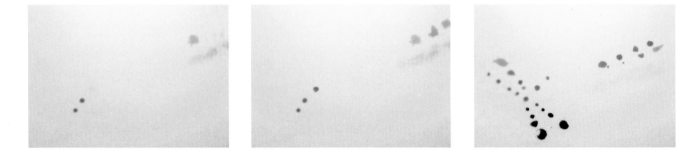

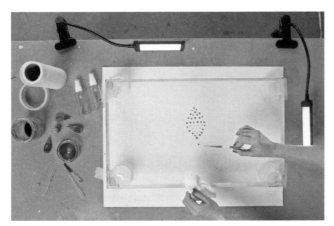

**fig. 1.** Put down a color drop with an eyedropper.

**fig. 2.** Pick up the color drop with a paper towel.

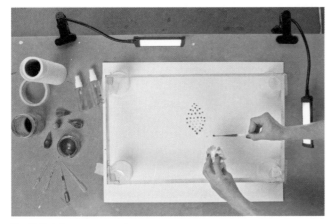

**fig. 3.** Put down a new color.

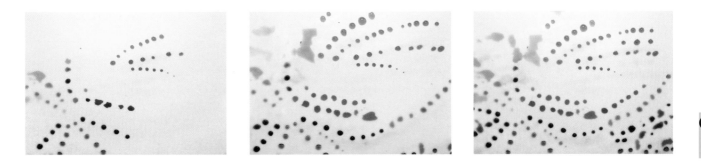

# SCROLLING
# BACKGROUNDS

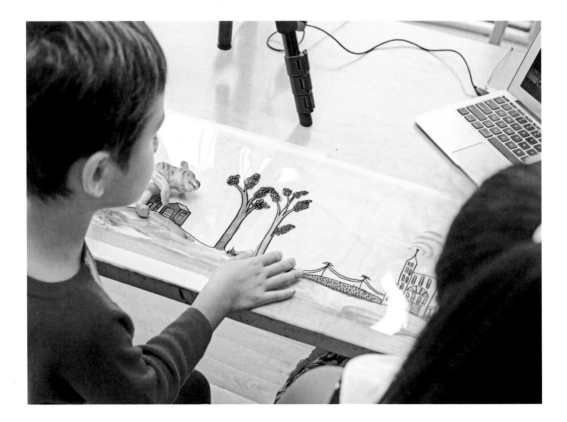

**This lab explores the exciting fun** of the scrolling backdrop as inspired by old favorite cartoons. While the background slowly scrolls by, a character or vehicle may bob along in one place, creating the illusion of forward motion. A complicated puppet can remain almost stationary while the backdrop itself does the moving! *Note:* Your camera (or capture device) will be in the "downshoot" style during this exercise (see page 62).

## BEFORE YOU BEGIN

- Plan your scene. Make a few sketches. Keep it simple to start. Once you have gotten the hang of this simple technique, you can create more complicated scenes and plotlines.

- What is the environment in which the action is taking place? This lab provides a great space for a character to take a tour through a changing world. Do you start in the desert and end in the city? Is the action taking place along a city street? If so, what kinds of buildings and street elements might we see?

- Take a moment to design your character or element that will be "moving" through these environments. Anything can be used as the moving element. Even a found object could be employed as the subject on the move (see Lab 12).

- Fine-tipped and fat-tipped permanent markers
- 2 to 4 long sheets of clear acetate cut to 11" (28 cm) tall by up to 30" (76 cm) long
- Acrylic paint or gouache
- Paintbrushes
- Camera or other capture device
- Tripod
- Masking tape

# ACTION!

**1** Using the permanent markers, draw your changing landscape in one long row on a sheet of clear acetate (fig. 1). Take time to consider how you will change one space into another. What is the progression of the drawing? What comes next in line? Imagine that you are on this journey yourself. What would you see next? Once you have designed the first scrolling background, perhaps you want to create a few more. Have at it!

**2** Now that you have "penned" (drawn in) the lines for your background, you can turn the acetate over and paint on the *back* from the underside (fig. 2). The permanent marker lines serve as guides that you can fill in using opaque paint. Acrylic paint and gouache (opaque watercolor) are great choices. Let the paint dry for 10–15 minutes.

**3** Finally, it's time to set up your shot! Once you have oriented your camera (remember to stabilize your capture device using a tripod or other rigging), use masking tape at the top and bottom of the acetate sheet to create a guideline along which to move the backdrop (fig. 3).

**4** Position the backdrop as far as you can on one end with the "moving" element in the middle of the scene. Now carefully pull the backdrop across the scene ever so slightly to reveal the next drawn area. The moving element should remain in relatively the same space in the frame throughout the entire animation, but it shouldn't simply remain still and lifeless. Try wobbling the subject back and forth slightly with each incremental scroll of the backdrop.

**5** When you have run out of backdrop, either feed in another strip or start over at the beginning! What a wonderful loop!

**fig. 1.** Draw the background on clear acetate using a permanent marker.

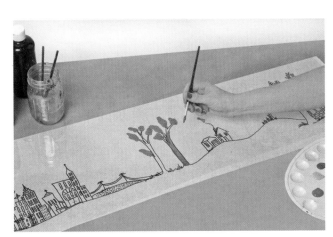

**fig. 2.** Fill in the drawn lines with paint on the reverse side.

**fig. 3.** Use masking tape as a guide for your moving background.

# TWO-DIMENSIONAL
# PUPPETS AND
# BACKDROPS

**This lab is an introduction** to a very versatile and fun way to make two-dimensional puppets for animating on a multiplane or any flat surface. We will also detail simple techniques to build backdrop elements to accompany your wonderful puppet. When you are through, you will have the building blocks to create a multiplane world that is full and multilayered!

## BEFORE YOU BEGIN

First, design your puppet using computer paper and a pencil. A little sketch will do. This character will take you through your first multiplane animation!

## MATERIALS

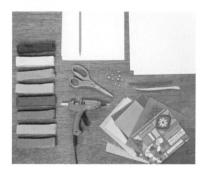

- Computer paper
- Pencil
- Heavyweight cardstock
- Scissors
- Non-hardening modeling clay in a variety of colors
- Clay sculpting tools
- Small round beads (preferably white)
- Patterned paper
- Hot glue gun (or liquid craft glue/glue stick)
- Masking tape
- Sheet of plexiglass (for multiplane)
- Camera or other capture device
- Tripod

# ACTION!

1 Once you have designed the puppet, you can begin building it! Using a heavyweight cardstock, draw your puppet again, but in separate pieces, considering which elements you would like to be movable and thus separate from each other. For instance, the arms and legs and head should be separate from the torso for a full range of motion. (Note: Creating too many intricate pieces can make for tricky animating.)

2 Cut out the pieces of your puppet (fig. 1).

3 This is where the real fun begins! Pinch off a tiny bit of modeling clay at a time and smear it on top of your cutout pieces (fig. 2). The clay can be shaped into lines, dots, squiggles—the sky is the limit! With the help of the clay sculpting tools, you can truly give your character a lot of personality and detail. Finally, add the beads for eyes with the center hole of the bead pointing up as though it were the pupil.

**animating tip** When you are working with this puppet and giving it expression and life, use a small pin or the end of a pencil inserted into the hole of the bead to gently turn the eyes a tiny bit at a time.

4 Now it's time to think about setting and environment! Because you will be animating on a flat surface, your set pieces can be flat, too. This frees you up to use a whole range of materials and methods! We love combining patterned papers to create interesting visual textures in our animated world. It also provides a nice contrast to the clay-covered puppet, but you could use any combination of fabric, felt, wire, or found objects, or even copy our clay-covered two-dimensional puppet technique for sets! (Note: Keep in mind the type of material that you are using when you select your glue: hot glue is great for heavier materials and can even be used on paper, though you might prefer a glue stick or liquid craft glue for some lighter materials.)

5 Use scissors to cut out simple shapes and glue them together to create a whole world (fig. 3). Keep in mind the scale of what you are creating: some of our favorite animated scenes have a lot of different sizes of set pieces in play. For example, some are very small for things in the distance (on a back layer of the multiplane) and some are quite large for the foreground (one of the topmost layers of the multiplane).

6 Use masking tape to affix your background to the plexiglass multiplane (fig. 4).

7 Set up your camera and tripod in the downshoot angle and have your character act out a scene.

**fig. 1.** Cut out the pieces of your puppet.

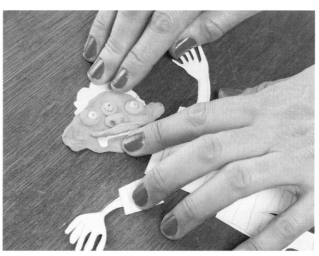

**fig. 2.** Smear modeling clay on the cut pieces of the puppet.

**fig. 3.** Glue together set pieces for a two-dimensional set.

**fig. 4.** Arrange your background on the multiplane, taping the pieces in place.

# EMILY COLLINS

Emily Collins is an animation director and partner at Mighty Oak, an animation studio located in Brooklyn, New York. Her animation work explores memory, abstract thought, and humor using cut paper, paint, pastels, and other tactile materials.

Emily was the recipient of a National Board of Review grant in 2015. Over the years, she has shown work at venues such as the Poetry Project at St. Mark's Church, Anthology Film Archives, Spectacle Theater, and the MUSMA Museum in Italy. She has collaborated on animation works with Penguin Books, the *New York Times*, Mashable, LEGO, and many others.

In 2013, she founded GirlStories, a free program for teen girls interested in film, comics, and animation located at the Children's Museum of the Arts in New York City. Emily holds a BFA in Film/Animation/Video from Rhode Island School of Design and an MFA in Integrated Media Arts from Hunter College.

Learn more at www.mightyoakgrows.com.

Still from a short tribute to the silhouette animation pioneer Lotte Reiniger. Featured by Mashable during Women's History Month. Made in 2016 at Mighty Oak.

Still from *Chula with Invisible Strings*, a Mighty Original short film.

Still from HATCH Stories, an original series about female founders. Made in 2016 at Mighty Oak.

# UNIT
# 4

# STRAIGHT-AHEAD ANIMATION

Straight-ahead animation is the art of animating anything with the camera pointing straight ahead at the subject rather than down at a tabletop. Thus, you are essentially animating in a three-dimensional world rather than a two-dimensional one (on a flat surface). Animating elements in the third dimension is a magical practice.

Before you begin the labs in this chapter, take a moment to consider that animating with a camera facing forward requires a secure area around your set and the tripod, and a space that's easy for you (the animator) to move and work within.

Also included in the labs that follow are some tricks to help you navigate a few classic challenges that animators experience when working in the third dimension.

# STRAIGHT-AHEAD CAMERA ANGLE

Beloved by most stop-motion animation moviemakers throughout the ages, the straight-ahead (or "three-dimensional") angle captures our world in all of its three-dimensional glory! Please note: This isn't "three-dimensional animation," where you create all images and movements on the computer. This is real-life filmmaking!

The straight-ahead camera angle is used in most stop-motion animation films that you see on the big screen today. This technique looks wonderful, but it does come with its share of technical challenges. Not to worry, these can be easily fixed with a good setup. Rigging and clever behind-the-scenes tricks will ensure that your straight-ahead angles will be truly impressive.

## Creating a Straight-Ahead Set

The basic requirements for the straight-ahead shoot—a film stage in the form of a table and some lighting—are the same as for a downshoot project (see page 63). Again, make sure your table measures at least 24 by 12 inches (61 by 30.5 cm) so you have enough room to work, and you should consider covering the top to avoid damage.

For straight-ahead projects, it's especially important to have clean, balanced lighting that lights your set and characters consistently.

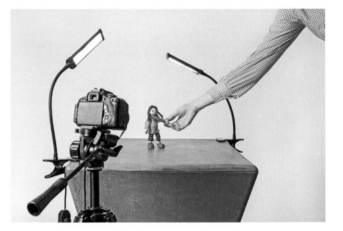

You can film a straight-ahead project with either a camera or a smartphone. Instead of a traditional tripod, you can use a frame-style tripod for your smartphone to give you a variety of shot options.

# MOTION ARCS

Motion arcs are simply guides that help you plan your movements in advance to make them more precise and strategic. In stop-motion animation terms, the most lifelike sequential movements tend to follow a curved path through space, or an arc. Creating "motion arcs" is a technique used by the pros to map out the course of an action. This trick is sure to make your puppets' moves smooth, slightly organic, slow, and even.

A motion arc feature is often included in professional-grade animation software, but it can also be imitated in real life by first marking your animation stage with points mapping where your animated actions should land. Try using something that cannot be detected by your camera, such as clear or matte transparent tape.

# PLAY WITH YOUR
# TOYS

**This lab helps animators** try their hand at working in a straight-ahead environment. It's also a great place to incorporate favorite toys or games right from their own world! To select materials, animators need look no further than their toy box or curio shelf.

### BEFORE YOU BEGIN

Make sure that you have a great space to animate in. You should have a surface on which to animate: this can be a tabletop or even the floor. Point the camera toward that general space and secure a backdrop behind your animation surface using masking tape. Now you have created a stage in which to animate! Also, it's a good idea to tape the feet of the tripod to the floor so that it won't move in case it gets bumped.

### MATERIALS

Note: *For this project, you will pick a variety of objects/toys to play with in front of the lens. Look for something large and flat that can serve as a backdrop; this can be an interesting piece of fabric, a poster, or a sign. You can also use a blank wall if you want a clean look.*

- Backdrop
- Camera or other capture device
- Tripod
- Lighting
- Masking tape
- Toys and objects

# ACTION!

1    Set up your backdrop, camera, tripod, and lighting, securing them with masking tape.

2    Arrange your objects in front of the lens (fig. 1). Take 15 pictures of your still environment with nothing moving. This sets a foundation for your film so that your audience has a moment for their eyes to adjust before things begin to move.

3    Next, move your elements a tiny bit. Remember that the smaller the movement, the smoother the motion will be. You can use the onion skin function on your stop-motion animation software to make sure that you are making small movements. Capture a photo of this change.

4    Repeat! Move your subjects bit by bit, taking photos each time (fig. 2).

5    Play with different types of movements. Try using small movements and also bigger movements. You could even place a new object in the same space that an old object was positioned in, creating a transformation. Try telling a simple story (fig. 3).

**fig. 1.** Arrange your objects in front of the camera.

**fig. 2.** Keep moving your objects a little at a time, taking pictures after each change.

**fig. 3.** Have your characters tell a simple story.

# HAND-SEWN
# THREE-DIMENSIONAL
# PUPPETS

**Design and make a poseable puppet** from start to finish: sketch your idea, shape the movable wire armature—your puppet's bone structure—cut and sew a fabric "skin," and then make it come alive!

## BEFORE YOU BEGIN

Before you can start building your puppet, you should explore and develop what it will look like, including its proportions (the size relationships among its body parts), in a few sketches using pencil on scratch paper. In addition to providing an opportunity to develop your drawing skills, this stage is for trying out and playing with different characters and looks. Your final sketch will serve as a guide to creating your puppet.

Once your sketch is complete, determine the size of your puppet so you'll know how much wire you'll need to cut for the armature. For a figure that stands about 8 inches (20.3 cm) tall—a recommended minimum height for animating in a small environment—you'll need about 30 inches (76.2 cm) of wire. If your puppet has any exaggerated features—for instance, a large head, or long arms or legs (or all three)—you'll need more wire.

## MATERIALS

- Pencil

- Scratch paper

- Wire cutters

- 32′ (9.8 m) spool of 16-gauge aluminum armature wire

- Needle-nose pliers

- 2 small wooden knobs or drawer pulls with flat fronts per puppet

- Masking tape

- Fabric

- Marker

- Ruler

- Straight pins

- Scissors

- Lightweight yarn and tapestry needle OR sewing needle and thread

- Buttons

- Non-hardening modeling clay or Sticky Tack (optional)

- Camera or other capture device

- Tripod

**1** Cut a 30-inch (76.2 cm) length of wire from the spool. As you create the puppet's armature, reference your sketch so you can shape the wire to reflect your design. To make the puppet's head, fold the wire in half, then twist a loop at the top (fig. 1). Use needle-nose pliers to hold the wire while twisting.

**2** To make an arm, fold over in a short loop one of the long pieces of wire descending beneath the head and then twist it (fig. 2). The end of that piece of wire will become one of the legs.

**3** Fold the longer piece of wire across the torso to form a loop on the other side. Twist the loop to form the other arm (fig. 3). You now have two arms and two legs.

**4** Wrap the wire at the base of each leg around a wooden knob to make feet and secure with masking tape (fig. 4). Make sure your puppet's legs are still long enough to allow for a broad range of movement.

**5** Fold the fabric in half so there are two layers, one on top of the other. Lay the armature with its arms and legs extended on top of the fabric and then trace with a marker. Leave at least 2 inches (5 cm) around it if you're using yarn to sew the fabric; you'll only need 1½ inches (3.8 cm) if you're using thread. Be sure to allow for extra space when tracing the wooden "feet"—think bell-bottom pants (fig. 5).

**6** Once you've finished tracing, set the armature aside. Pin the two pieces of fabric so the layers stay together, then cut along your traced guidelines (fig. 6).

**7** Start sewing around the right half of the skin—the right ankle is a great place to start—continuing just over the head and stopping at the left shoulder so you can slip the armature in with ease. Continue sewing around the fabric until your puppet is completely covered. Do *not* cover the wooden feet with fabric—they should remain exposed for easy animating (fig. 7).

**8** Give your puppet a face. Buttons and beads make great eyes and noses, or you can draw or paint a face.

**9** For extra stability and support, use non-hardening modeling clay or Sticky Tack to stick your puppet's feet to the tabletop. Set up your camera and tripod. Now your puppet is ready for action (fig. 8)!

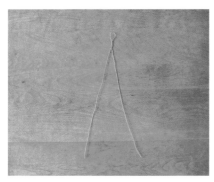

**fig. 1.** Fold, loop, and twist the wire to make the head.

**fig. 2.** Fold over one piece of wire across the other and make a loop. Twist the loop of wire to form an arm.

**fig. 3.** Using the longer piece of wire, fold it up across the torso and make a loop. Twist the loop into the second arm.

**fig. 4.** Twist the bottom of each leg around a wooden knob to make sturdy feet and secure with masking tape.

**fig. 5.** Trace the outline of the armature onto the fabric, leaving space around it for sewing.

**fig. 6.** Pin the fabric together and then cut along the traced lines.

**fig. 7.** Sew the fabric skin around the armature, leaving the wooden feet exposed.

**fig. 8.** Add a face and then make your puppet move!

# THREE-DIMENSIONAL
# CLAYMATION PUPPETS

# These puppets are such fun to make and animate!

Animators can try their hand at sketching, sculpting, and even a little fashion design!

## BEFORE YOU BEGIN

As with the fabric puppet (Lab 14), take a moment to design what you would like your puppet to look like. You will be using a greater variety of materials to create this puppet, so you can do more with facial features and details. Use some scratch paper to try out a few ideas. Think about proportions, materials you might use for clothing, hair, and how you will design those clay features. Again, your final sketch will serve as a guide to creating your puppet.

For this lab, we will be using the same measuring technique that we used for the fabric puppet. Determine the size of your puppet so you'll know how much wire you'll need to cut for the armature. Refer to steps 1 to 3 in Lab 14 to create the wire armature.

- Pencil
- Scratch paper
- Wire cutters
- 32' (9.8 m) spool of 16-gauge aluminum armature wire
- Needle-nose pliers
- Aluminum foil
- Masking tape
- Fabric
- Marker
- Straight pins
- Scissors
- Hot glue gun
- Non-hardening modeling clay in a variety of colors
- Clay sculpting tools
- Beads for eyes
- Yarn for hair (optional)
- Camera or other capture device
- Tripod

# ACTION!

1. Follow steps 1 through 3 in Lab 14 to make the puppet's armature, leaving large loops on the ends for the hands and feet.

2. Rip off strips of aluminum foil and wrap them loosely around the armature, bunching up areas to give more mass (fig. 1).

3. Wrap the foil with masking tape so that it is secure (fig. 2).

4. Fold the fabric in half so that there are two layers, one on top of the other. Lay the armature with its arms and legs extended on top of the fabric and trace around it with a marker to create clothing (fig. 3).

5. Set aside the armature, pin the fabric together, and then cut it out.

6. Lay the covered armature on the back panel of the outfit and glue it down using the hot glue gun. Next, glue on the top panel, creating complete coverage (fig. 4). Remember to leave the feet free of fabric. Clay puppets do well with large feet that stick to surfaces and animate easily.

7. Now let's add clay features. We want to keep the puppet fairly light in its upper half so that it is easy to pose and won't slump over during the course of your animation.

    Use clay sculpting tools to help create features and fine lines. Beads work well as eyes. Also add the hands and feet (fig. 5).

8. Cover the head in hair. Yarn works well and can be easily attached with the hot glue gun (fig. 6). Or you can use other types of materials for hair, such as paper, clay, or wire.

9. Lastly, make sure the feet are stable. You may need to cover the feet with another layer of modeling clay and shape them so the puppet will stand upright (fig. 7).

10. Now you're ready to set up your camera and tripod and snap away!

**fig. 1.** Wrap aluminum foil around the armature to create the body.

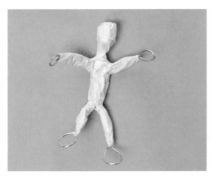

**fig. 2.** Wrap the foil armature with masking tape.

**fig. 3.** Trace the outline of the armature onto the fabric, leaving space around it for gluing.

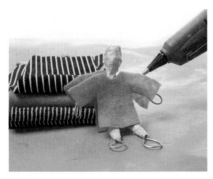

**fig. 4.** Adhere the clothing to the body with a hot glue gun.

**fig. 5.** Create a face, hands, and feet with modeling clay.

**fig. 6.** Attach hair to the puppet's head.

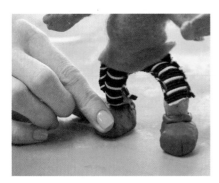

**fig. 7.** Shape the feet with more modeling clay so they're stable and will hold the puppet upright.

# THREE-DIMENSIONAL
# CLAYMATION TREES

**Let's add to your animation environment.** This extra set piece helps create a unique world—and it's also movable!

## MATERIALS

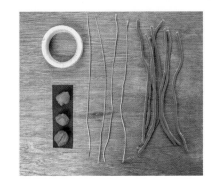

– Wire cutters
– 32′ (9.8 m) spool of 16-gauge aluminum armature wire
– Pipe cleaners
– Needle-nose pliers
– Masking tape
– Non-hardening modeling clay in brown
– Clay sculpting tools

# ACTION!

1. Decide how tall you would like your tree to be, considering that the base of your tree will be made of "roots" that you will secure to a tabletop. Cut 5 to 8 lengths of armature wire that are more or less equal lengths. Cut the pipe cleaners into 4 similar lengths.

2. Twist together the lengths of wire in the center, creating a trunk with loose wire at the top and the bottom. Wrap the branches and trunk with masking tape, creating a stable armature (fig. 1). Build up certain areas to create variations in shape and texture.

3. To make the leaves, gather the pipe cleaners and twist them together. Cut into short lengths about 1 to 2 inches (2.5 to 5 cm) long (fig. 2). Play with the pipe cleaners to make different kinds of foliage. Does your tree have wild, curly leaves like ours, or short, spiky leaves?

4. Tape the wire roots to the tabletop for stability. Wrap your pipe cleaner leaves around the ends of the branches in small bunches. Add modeling clay to the armature in a thin layer (fig. 3).

**fig. 1.** Cut wire lengths to the desired size and then twist the wires together to form a trunk and branches. Wrap the armature with tape.

**fig. 2.** To make leaves, twist four pipe cleaners together and cut into short lengths.

**fig. 3.** Attach pipe cleaners to the branches and apply modeling clay to the trunk.

# LAB
# 17

# LEARNING TO FLY:
# WORKING WITH RIGGING

**This lab leads you through** a helpful method that enables puppets to fly in a straight-ahead angle or three-dimensional environment. Having some fishing line on hand is always a great place to start, but even though the support method is invisible, it can be hard to hold your puppet still in space because the fishing line tends to swing and sway slightly. Following these steps ensures a stable holding technique that is still transparent to the camera's lens.

## MATERIALS

- Puppet, toy, or found object of your choosing
- Length of clear plastic dowel, either round or square and at least ³⁄₁₆" (4.8 mm) in diameter
- Large binder clips, masking tape, or thin wire
- Camera or other capture device
- Tripod
- Set to house the action

## ACTION!

**1** Securely attach your puppet to the end of the clear plastic dowel using a binder clip, masking tape, or thin wire.

**2** Hold the clear plastic dowel at one end just out of sight of the camera and carefully move your puppet into the set through the air. Capture each incremental movement with the camera.

**3** Your puppet can fly!

# LOOKS LIKE
# WATER

**This lab tackles one of the most challenging tricks** in animation: creating believable water! The tricky thing is that you need a substance that looks fluid but can hold a position until you are ready for it to move. Using some simple materials, you will be able to create a small set complete with a magic watering hole!

- Masking tape
- Tray for holding body of "water"
- Recycled cardboard boxes and/or plastic cups to create height in your set
- Paper towels
- Large sheets of felt or fabric
- Scissors
- Hot glue gun
- Natural or natural-looking materials, such as moss, rocks, and sticks
- Shells and/or river rocks
- Blue hair gel
- Camera or other capture device
- Tripod

## ACTION!

1   Tape the tray to a tabletop, where you will be animating (fig. 1).

2   Arrange the cardboard boxes and/or plastic cups around the tray, imagining that they are hills around the magic watering hole. Tape down the items securely to the table when you have put them in a place that you are happy with. Add bunched-up paper towels to create a more rounded shape.

3   Next, lay large sheets of felt or fabric down on top of the boxes, cutting and trimming as you see fit. Hot glue these sheets down to the items to make hills (fig. 2).

4   Position your materials on your hills and around the watering hole. Use the hot glue gun to attach these securely as well (fig. 3).

5   Place a thin layer of shells and/or river rocks in the tray (fig. 4).

6   To add "water," pour the blue hair gel into the tray on top of the shells and/or river rocks (fig. 5). Now you're ready to set up your camera and tripod and animate (fig. 6)!

**fig. 1.** Tape down your "watering hole" tray.

**fig. 2.** Hot glue the felt or fabric to the recycled materials.

**fig. 3.** Add natural (or natural-looking) materials to your landscape.

**fig. 4.** Add river rocks and shells to your watering hole.

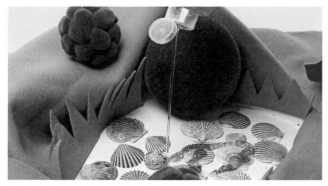

**fig. 5.** Add blue hair gel to look like water.

**fig. 6.** Set up a diving board so your puppet can go swimming!

# MEET THE ANIMATOR

# HAYLEY MORRIS

Hayley Morris is a director, an artist, and an animator based in New York City and Providence, Rhode Island, where she teaches stop-motion animation at her alma mater, the Rhode Island School of Design (RISD). Her company, Shape & Shadow, is a full-service animation studio that uses traditional animation techniques such as stop-motion and hand drawing to tell stories that unfold through layered textures, handcrafted details, and experimentation. Hayley creates her animations using many different art and craft media, including paper, fabric, and clay.

Hayley has directed commercials for companies including Burt's Bees, Samsung, HumanaOne, Kate Spade, and the Detroit Zoo; has worked as an animator and a fabricator on commercials for Special K, McDonald's, Toyota, the *New York Times*, Cadbury, and many other brands; and has created music videos for the singer-songwriter Iron & Wine as well as for the pianist Hauschka and Grammy Award–winning violinist Hilary Hahn. Hayley's work has been featured at film festivals and museums around the world. Her short film *Undone* won the Grand Jury Prize for Best Animated Short at Slamdance in 2009. More recently, her sets, puppets, and music videos were shown at La Gaîté Lyrique's "Motion Factory" exhibit in Paris, which showcased the work of fifteen directors from around the world who create handmade films in the digital age. To see more of Hayley's work, visit www.hayleymorris.net.

Top: Hayley Morris works on a paper bird puppet for *Bounce Bounce,* a stop-motion music video for a collaboration between Hauschka and Hilary Hahn. Most of the action takes place underwater and features dancing sea creatures (center and bottom).

Whimsical paper structures from the music video "Dream the Dare," a song written and performed by the band Pure Bathing Culture, from their album *Moon Tides*.

Both the butterfly and the image on its wings are animated in the music video for the song "Joy" by Iron & Wine, from his album *Ghost on Ghost*.

A scene of figures farming crops against a backdrop of Aztec temples is constructed entirely from paper. From the short film *Seed: The Untold Story*.

In the animated short film *Undone,* a polymer clay puppet fishes in a sea of fabrics in various shades of blue.

# PIXILATION

The original roots of "movie magic" are truly revealed in this unit. From the early days of cinema, when audiences were dazzled by viewing the seemingly impossible on the screen, these behind-the-scenes tricks now make their way into our lab investigating the art of pixilation, or the technique of animating a human or other living subject.

As you have discovered in previous chapters and labs, stop-motion animation gives us a wonderful opportunity to manipulate our subjects or scenes in between photos, creating the illusion of motion, transformation, and more. In the following labs, you can try your hands (and bodies) at animating yourselves in short film form. Become the magician you always wanted to be! Sleight-of-hand tricks have never been so easy.

# MOVIE MAGIC
# TRANSFORMATIONS

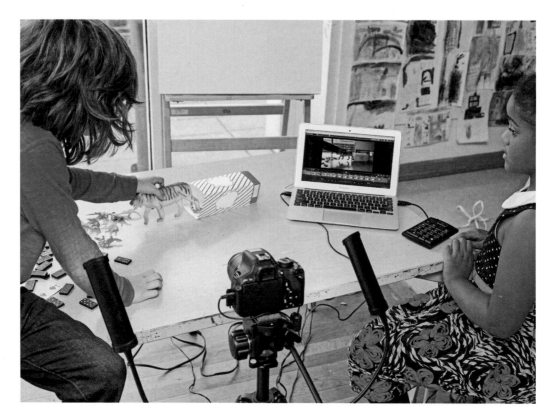

**This lab introduces some simple transformation** tricks as well as the technique of using your hands as animate-able elements in a short film. Just using your hands is a great way to jump into what's possible through pixilation!

*Note:* Kids who are practicing their fine motor skills will be challenged by this lab, because it's essential that they use slow and measured movements for the animation to appear smooth. This lab is better with a team of at least two kids, so one can animate with her hands and the other can operate the camera or animation software.

## BEFORE YOU BEGIN

First set up your camera in a straight-ahead position pointed toward a tabletop (which will serve as your animation stage). Add a backdrop using a large piece of paper or fabric, or just shoot in front of a blank wall. Start with an empty space and a box, or "transformation chamber."

## MATERIALS

Note: *The focus of this lab is transformation, so start with a prop that you have lying around the house or that can be bought in multiples. Examples include dice, dominoes, playing cards, packs of small plastic toys, a bag of wrapped candy, or stacks of plastic cups. And don't forget the most important animate-able material: YOU!*

- Camera or other capture device
- Tripod
- Backdrop (optional)
- Box for a "transformation chamber"
- Animation props

## ACTION!

**1** Slowly move your hand in small, incremental movements, bringing your hand into view of the camera. Slowly move your hand (remember to capture photos of each move!) so that you go from a relaxed pose to one where you are pointing toward the box, or "transformation chamber."

**2** While holding your hand as steady as possible, carefully place one of your animation props facing the box (fig. 1). Now capture that new image. Your hand has now become a magic wand! Play with all of the different ways that you can make things appear in the scene.

**3** Now, let's experiment with making your prop transform! Again, using your pointer finger as a magic wand, slowly move your prop into the box. Now, holding your "magic" hand totally still, replace the element with a new one, coming out of the box (fig. 2). Now capture that new image. Repeat this transformation technique with all of your props.

**4** Time for some disappearing acts! Once again, use that magic hand to slowly approach each element one small movement at a time. Try something different for your grand finale: perhaps executing a slow-motion snap of the fingers. At the same time that you snap, hold your hand completely still and remove the element nearest to your hand. Now, slowly repeat, moving your hand over an element, slow-motion snapping, and removing!

**5** If you are using animation software, you might consider animating at 10 frames per second rather than 15. The movements in pixilation are often more difficult to control, so a lower frame speed will allow for a slightly slower pace.

**fig. 1.** Use your hands to magically make a prop appear near your "transformation chamber."

**fig. 2.** A newly transformed prop comes out of the "transformation chamber."

# PIXILATED OLYMPICS

**Pixilation reaches new athletic feats** during this tour through what is possible using our bodies as animate-able elements! This is great for kids who are practicing their gross motor skills, and it is fun to include many kids at once, as this project gets physical.

## MATERIALS

- Camera or other capture device
- Tripod
- Large piece of fabric
- Yourselves!

## ACTION*!*

### Flying

**1** Ever wanted to fly? Here's your chance! By jumping in the air and capturing each photo at just the right moment, you will appear to be in flight. First, turn the camera so that it is facing forward toward your subject. Have the director ready to take photos and direct the flying subject. The director should count "1, 2, 3, jump!" and the subject should jump as high as she can on the command "jump!" and keep her arms at her sides (see opposite). The goal is to capture the very moment when the subject's feet are off the ground.

**2** Repeat this action again, but this time with the subject's arms up in the air, like wings (fig. 1).

**3** Keep repeating steps 1 and 2 again and again (using the commands "1, 2, 3, jump!" "1, 2, 3, jump!" "1, 2, 3, jump!") and capture each jump on film—the subject will appear to be in flight.

**fig. 1.** Jump, lifting your arms in the air. It will look like you are flying.

**fig. 2.** The landing!

## Swimming

1 Set up the camera and tripod so that they are facing down toward the floor. Allow for a clear and large space directly below the camera so that the animators can comfortably move their arms and legs in wide arcs while lying on the floor without hitting or disturbing the camera/tripod.

2 Lay the large piece of fabric down on the floor within view of the camera.

3 Now, one person will be the camera/animation software director and another will be an Olympic swimmer. The swimmer lies on the floor on top of the fabric and slowly mimics the movements of swimming a tiny bit at a time while the director captures each photo (fig. 3). Try tricks like doing slow-motion flips (the subject may need to actually get up and lie back down between each photo so that the backdrop fabric stays fairly still through the process). Also, the backdrop fabric can be swirled and moved frame by frame to mimic water.

**fig. 3.** Swimming in a striped sea

### Skating

1 What a fun exercise this one is! It's great for helping kids develop gross motor skills and balance. In this lab, participants will be able to magically skate on solid ground. First, position your camera toward your subjects. Again, have a director on hand to take the photos and to help them find and hold the proper positions along the way. Practice standing on one foot to work on balance before you begin taking photos (fig. 4).

2 Now have your "skaters" decide which foot they will stand on as each photo is captured. Once you are ready, have your skaters stand on one foot, balancing with the other bent behind them: take a picture! Now have your skaters take a tiny step forward and return to their skating position, standing on the same foot: take a picture! Repeat again and again until your skaters have to take a break. When you play back your film, it will appear that your actors are skating magically on one foot without any effort!

**fig. 4.** Synchronized skaters

# LAB
# 21

# COOKING IOI:
# ANIMATED MEALS

**This is a culinary take** on pixilation transformations that will come out as a real feast! Using a variety of materials mixed up together in one pot will create the illusion of a cooking project, and the resulting short film is sure to satisfy your appetite. As with our other pixilation labs, this one is most easily accomplished with the help of a friend or collaborator who can be the director taking photos while another person creates the recipe.

## BEFORE YOU BEGIN

Set your stage. Angle the camera toward your animation environment in a shot that will show your arms and cooking set OR point the camera down so that you can see the inside of the pot and your hands positioned above.

## MATERIALS

- Camera or other capture device
- Tripod
- Bubble wrap
- Cooking tools to be used as props: pots and pans, spoons, whisk, tongs, cheese grater, etc.
- Found objects in multiples, such as googly eyes, pipe cleaners, dice, dominoes, candy, or beads

# ACTION!

1   Start with bubble wrap lining the inside of your cooking pot to look like boiling water. After taking your introductory 15 photos to set a foundation, begin moving the bubble wrap a little bit at a time, capturing each movement with a photo.

2   Next, moving in very small, incremental motions, add a new material to your pot.

3   Repeat step 2, using different cooking implements to add new "ingredients" to the pot (figs. 1 and 2).

4   From here, it is up to you to play, replace, transform, and combine ingredients to make a masterful meal. The only thing to remember is that you must make small movements and capture photos of those movements!

**fig. 1.** Use tongs to add some bendable pipe cleaners.

**fig. 2.** "Grate" some dice into the pot to transform them into dominos.

# PES

PES is the creator of some of the most widely viewed stop-motion films of all time, including *KaBoom!, Game Over, Human Skateboard, Western Spaghetti*, and *Fresh Guacamole*. On YouTube alone, his films have been viewed more than 150 million times.

PES's uncanny knack for transforming familiar objects through stop-motion animation has earned him global recognition and dozens of honors, including an Academy Award nomination for *Fresh Guacamole* in 2013. (It is the shortest film ever nominated for an Oscar.) In addition to his original content, PES has directed more than fifty commercials for major international brands, including Google, Honda, Orange Telecom, Kinder Surprise, PlayStation, Sprint, Samsung, and Bacardi. You can see more of PES's work by visiting http://pesfilm.com.

Still from *Submarine Sandwich*

(below) Stills from *Fresh Guacamole*

(below) Stills from *Western Spaghetti*

# GLOSSARY

**Abstract:** A type of art that uses colors and lines to express emotions and ideas rather than concrete pictures or events.

**Acetate:** A clear sheet of plastic film that can be purchased at crafts stores, office supply stores, and art stores.

**Angle:** The position of a camera as related to its mount on a tripod.

**Animation:** A movie-making technique that uses a series of graphics, photographs, drawings, paintings, handmade puppets, or three-dimensional printed models.

**Armature:** The metal skeleton of a puppet or sculpture, which is then covered with fabric or clay.

**Backdrop:** The background of a set, often a piece of cloth or paper painted to look like the area in which the action takes place, such as outdoors or in a room.

**Bird's Eye:** A type of shot taken from high above, as if from the point of view of a bird in the sky.

**Camera:** A tool used for recording pictures and movies. With today's technology, a camera can be as simple as a smartphone or as advanced as professional photography equipment.

**Cel:** Short for "celluloid," a piece of clear film that can be drawn on as in classic cartoon production. We use this traditional technique in Lab 6, but not the same material.

**Character:** A person or other subject who is a part of a story either as the main focus or in a supporting role.

**Charcoal:** A black, chalk-like material used in art for lines and shading.

**Claymation:** A stop-motion animation technique that features clay figures as the subjects.

**Close-Up:** A type of camera shot that highlights details or showcases the emotions and facial expressions of a character. An "Extreme Close-Up" is even closer.

**Copyright:** Laws that protect the creative work of an artist. Materials, such as music and images, under copyright may not be used without permission.

**Downshoot Camera Angle:** A type of production setup in which the camera is pointed down toward the ground, a tabletop, or any other flat surface. This angle is used for a wide range of animation techniques, including those where gravity poses a problem, such as puppetry, and creates a two-dimensional effect.

**Editing:** Part of the postproduction process, the act of arranging images, adding sound and text, and putting other finishing touches on the film.

**Film Stage:** The surface on which a scene is set up. We suggest a no-frills table with a top measuring at least 24 by 12 inches (61 by 30.5 cm).

**Flip Book:** A collection of pages featuring slightly different images so that when they are turned quickly, the pictures seem to have movement. The more pages, the smoother the animation will appear. We recommend 15 to 24 frames per movement for a good range of motion.

**Foley:** The process of creating and sourcing everyday sounds for a film, such as footsteps and creaking doors.

**Incremental:** Making small changes to something at a gradual, evenly-spaced pace.

**Lens:** The part of a camera that collects light and converts the image in focus into a photo.

**Light Box:** A desk-like tool with a flat plastic or glass surface that can be lit from underneath to help make tracing and copying frames easier.

**Lighting:** Equipment that produces light; or the arrangement of lights to create a certain effect. In this book, we recommend at least two direct light sources to create balance.

**Loop:** A sequence that starts and ends at the same place.

**Medium (angle):** A type of camera shot that combines information with a clearer focus on detail. Often used to capture conversational moments.

**Medium (art):** A material used to create a piece of art, or the method an artist uses. The plural of "medium" in this case is "media."

**Motion Arcs:** Guides that help to map out the course of an action to make it more precise and strategic. In stop-motion animation, the most lifelike movements tend to follow a curved path through space, or an arc.

**Multiplanes:** A stack of plexiglass with space between each sheet, giving more than one surface on which to work and creating the illusion of depth.

**Narrative:** A story, which is made up of plot, theme, characters, settings, conflict, and so on.

**Onion Skin Function:** A common tool in editing software programs that layers the last photo taken over the one about to be taken so that it's easier to plan the next move.

**Over the Shoulder:** A type of camera shot used to record the back and forth of a conversation or to show a character's unique perspective.

**Pan:** A type of camera shot that slowly moves along a straight line, taking photos of each incremental change.

**Penned:** Drawn in, such as lines for a background.

**Perspective:** Point of view; or balancing the proportions of objects in relation to each other's size, height, and position when seen from a certain angle.

**Pixilation:** A style of stop-motion animation with humans or other living beings as the subjects.

**Postproduction:** Work done after filming and photography has finished, such as editing, adding sounds, and putting scenes in the right order.

**Public Domain:** Creative materials, such as music or images, not protected by copyright laws and therefore free and available for use.

**Production:** The process of making a film, including setting scenes, adding subjects, and photography.

**Rigging:** Equipment, such as fishing line and dowels, that enables puppets to fly in a straight-ahead angle or three-dimensional environment.

**Scene:** A segment of a film that contains action and moves the story forward.

**Script:** A written document containing the words characters say and directions for their emotions or movements.

**Scrolling Backdrop:** A long background that can be slowly moved, creating the illusion of forward motion even though the character or vehicle in front of it remains still.

**Sequence:** A series of scenes or shots that depend on one another. A film may be shot out of sequence to eliminate switching out sets and resetting up a scene.

**Set:** The stage on which the action will take place.

**Shot:** A camera or software trick used to shape a scene. Examples include a close-up, wide shot, or pan.

**Shot List:** A written plan of the essential shots (animated moments) needed to make a story complete.

**Sound:** The part of a film that can be heard, such as everyday noises, speaking, or music.

**Stop-Motion Animation:** A type of film making during which action happens in real life, not constructed in a computer. Subjects and sets are incrementally manipulated by animators and photographed, creating the illusion of movement.

**Storyboard:** A visual aid outlining a story and breaking down each scene to plan for camera shots, select camera angles, and create shot lists.

**Straight-Ahead Camera Angle:** A type of production setup in which the camera is pointed forward, rather than pointing down, creating a three-dimensional world.

**Subject:** A person or thing being focused on and animated.

**Three-Dimensional:** An image or object that has length, width, and depth. In this book, "three-dimensional" refers to real-life filmmaking, not computer-generated images and movements.

**Title Cards:** Text that introduces a film and closes a film, such as the title, the name of the production company, and the names of people who participated in the project.

**Tripod:** A stand, typically with three legs, on which a camera can be mounted to make sure each shot is steady and focused.

**Two-Dimensional:** An image or object that has length and width, but no depth; flat. In animation, the down-shoot camera angle is most often used.

**Viewpoint:** Or point of view, the place from which a story is presented.

**Voice-Over:** Narration, or spoken words, added to a film even though the speaker is not shown on screen.

**Wide:** A type of camera shot that shows the subject as well as its surroundings to convey a lot of information at once.

**Worm's Eye:** A type of camera shot taken from the ground pointing upward into space, as if from the point of view of a worm.

**Zoetrope:** Literally "wheel of life," a term coined by William F. Lincoln for his cylindrical "moving picture" device. It is created by cutting vertical slits into the sides of a cylinder, the inside of which features a band of sequential images that when spun creates the illusion of motion.

**Zoom:** A type of camera shot that slowly expands or contracts the lens to move from a close-up angle to a wide angle or the other way around.

# RESOURCES

## Technical Guidance

Animation Physics
animationphysics.org

DragonFrame
dragonframe.com

Freesound
freesound.org

iKITMovie
ikitmovie.com

iMovie
www.apple.com/mac/
imovie

## Communities and Helpful Information

The 11 Second Club
11secondclub.com

Animate Clay
animateclay.com

Animation Magazine
animationmagazine.net

Animation World Network
awn.com/animationworld

Brickfilms
brickfilms.com

Cartoon Brew
cartoonbrew.com

Clay Animator
clayanimator.com

Great Women Animators
greatwomenanimators.
com

Stop Motion Central
stopmotioncentral.com

Toon Boom
toonboom.com

## Museums

AniMagic
Lee, Massachusetts, USA
mambor.com/animagic

Cartoon Art Museum
San Francisco, California,
USA
cartoonart.org

Museum of the Moving
Image
Astoria, New York, USA
movingimage.us

National Media Museum
Bradford, West Yorkshire,
England
www.nationalmediamu-
seum.org.uk/planavisit/
exploreourgalleries/
animationgallery

## Festivals

Anima
Brussels, Belgium
animatv.be

Internationales Trickfilm
Festival (Festival of
Animated Film)
Stuttgart, Germany
itfs.de

London International
Animation Festival
liaf.org.uk

New York International
Children's Film Festival
nyicff.org

## Influential Artists and Studios

*These are just a few of the many amazing artists and studios, past and present. Check them out and get inspired!*

Aardman
aardman.com

Becky and Joe
beckyandjoes.com

Bruce Bickford
brucebickford.com

Tim Burton
timburton.com

Art Clokey
premavision.com

David Daniels
stratacut.com

Ray Harryhausen
harryhausen.com

LAIKA
laika.com

Norman McLaren
mclarenwalltowall.com

Allison Schulnik
allisonschulnik.com

Suzie Templeton
suzietempleton.com

## Further Reading

*Animation: The Whole Story* by Howard Beckerman. New York: Allworth Press, 2003.

*The Animator's Survival Kit* by Richard Williams. New York: Faber & Faber, 2012.

*The World History of Animation* by Stephen Cavalier. Berkeley, CA: University of California Press, 2011.

# CONTRIBUTING ARTISTS

**Emily Collins**
www.mightyoakgrows.com

**Kirsten Lepore**
www.kirstenlepore.com

**Hayley Morris**
www.hayleymorris.net

**PES**
http://pesfilm.com

# ACKNOWLEDGMENTS

How thankful we are to acknowledge the people who helped this book become a reality. First we would like to thank Joy Aquilino, acquiring editor at Quarry Books, for coming to us with the idea of turning our daily work with students into a book that could move far beyond our small reach. Her encouragement and insight along the way was invaluable. We would also like to give a warm thank you to Jesse Untracht-Oakner, our brilliant photographer and faithful friend. Thank you for jumping in with us and for the grace you gave us as we navigated the uncharted territory of writing a book. Many, many, many thanks to our amazing teaching artists we have the pleasure of working with at The Good School. Your dedication, passion, and creativity inspire us every day. The work you do is important, and we are so thankful for you. And lastly, we would like to thank our faithful TGS students, families, and partners. You make this all possible, and you make it all oh so fun. It is truly good work.

# ABOUT THE AUTHORS

**Laura Bellmont** and **Emily Brink** are the co-founders and lead teachers of **The Good School**, an arts education school that cultivates and combines traditional art-making skills and the technologies involved in stop-motion animation filmmaking. They teach animation techniques at camps, schools, and events, including the New York International Children's Film Festival. They also offer professional development for teachers, including those at The Met, Spence School, and Pratt Institute.

### Laura

A trained illustrator and arts educator, Laura has served children and adults in the New York area for over ten years. She is passionate about progressive arts education and has found a perfect mobile venue for her love of teaching in the formation of The Good School. Laura received her Bachelors of Fine Arts in Illustration as well as her MS in Art + Design Education from Pratt Institute, graduating from both programs with honors.

### Emily

A professional graphic designer and arts educator, Emily has been working in New York City since 2010. She believes that by inviting today's youth into the rich world of art-making through the process of animation, she can help create a new generation of problem solvers, culture makers, and intelligent consumers who have the potential to bring creative change to all spheres of influence. Emily received her BFA in Visual Communications from the University of Oklahoma and her MS in Art + Design Education from Pratt Institute, where she graduated with honors.

# INDEX